UNDERSTANDING SOCIALISM AND THE DANGER IT BRINGS

A BASIC PRIMER

Rev. Dr. Melvin L. Johnson

PAGE PUBLISHING
Conneaut Lake, PA

First originally published by Page Publishing 2024

ISBN 979-8-89157-605-6 (pbk)
ISBN 979-8-89157-647-6 (digital)

Printed in the United States of America

Acknowledgments

First and above all, I want to thank God my Father who gave me life, Jesus who saved it, and the Holy Spirit who keeps it. Then I thank God for my beautiful and forever-youthful wife, Sheena, who has learned to endeavor with me for these forty-two years. You have cared for and nurtured many and the children do call you blessed.

I am also grateful to the members of the Heart of Christ Community Church family for trusting me with their spiritual nurturing and care as your undershepherd, a calling not to be unappreciated or taken lightly.

Last but not least of all, in recognizing that our freedom is a gift that must be paid for periodically by you—our veterans—I offer first a great salute and honor you with the greatest amount of respect and appreciation. Our remaining WWII veterans helped to shape our nation and lives in a way that enabled us to live, grow and prosper. But I also am compelled to not just honor our Korean and Vietnam War veterans and heroes, but also offer each of you a sympathetic and tearful apology from us here in America letting you down. I would not have had to write this book if we had stayed vigilant in to guard our communities, cultures, and institutions against this Marxist movement running uncontrollably today. The thirty-six thousand American soldiers we lost in Korea and the fifty-eight thousand warriors we lost in Vietnam died fighting on those distant shores in order to stop them from reaching our shores. Unfortunately we have basically failed up to this point.

Lesson Objectives

At the end of these lessons, the individual should be able to:

1. Describe the ways that ungodly people seek to remove the references to God and express their extreme hatred for him.
2. Describe the meaning of morality and intelligently discuss the differences between God's and man's.
3. Discuss how the phrase in Acts 4:35 can be easily substituted by Karl Marx's "Gotha Slogan" and then used within the Christian environment.
4. Explain why socialists must have a victim class in order to gain traction and maintain credibility.
5. Explain why lying and deception are seen to be positive character traits and strategies under the socialist model for effective leadership and governance.
6. Explain why socialism and Christianity are incompatible and cannot coexist.
7. Describe what it is like to live in a purely socialist, government-controlled system.
8. Explain why the final solution within a socialistic system is death.

Introduction

The Berlin Wall was infamously known as "The Iron Curtain."

What used to lurk in the shadows and the darkness of night now parades down main street in broad daylight! There was a time when the word called *socialism* had all but evaporated from the normal and regular conversation across the fruited plain. In short, let us first establish a ground rule as far as language and terminology is concerned. For starters, socialism is the entry way into communism. It may take merely a few years as it did with Hugo Chavez's Venezuelan debacle, or it may take decades as with much of western Europe, as countries such as France begins to experience increasingly greater unrest among its citizenry because of system failures. So when the terms socialism or socialist are mentioned, please recognize that they are closely related to communism and communist. More details will be explained later.

After the Korean War, the United States unceremoniously ended its second military conflict against communism through the Vietnam War. Many of our soldiers returned home to America with their personal issues following them and with new issues confronting them. Obviously, our national focus began to shift from the far east to the middle east as we became concerned about the encroaching dangers of Organization of Petroleum Exporting Countries (OPEC), and its effect upon the gas pump as well as the struggle to perform a balance act with the cultural revolution consisting of drug abuse, civil rights, and sexual promiscuity to name a few.

It had been barely a little more than thirty years passing at that time since the closure of the military interests of the Vietnam War, but the terms *socialism* and *communism* had already begun to evaporate from the minds of the overwhelming majority of most Americans. Besides, as the last of the Baby Boomers began to become more entrenched and focused on being the "establishment," Islam became our focus.

We became paralyzed with the terror in terrorism. The certain and determinate willingness of a Muslim to die for the Islamic faith, and the unquestionably mystical power of the ayatollahs and Islamic leaders of the Middle East in general, even challenged us to examine how devoted were we to our own Christian beliefs. Was there any other religious system with the power and influence to create armies of faithful believers who love their faith to the point of self-sacrifice? This religious devotion had awakened us to a danger that was eminent and could not be ignored. Vietnam was nearly two generations ago, distant and quite vague to the millennials, but the Islamic world had reached into and jolted the very heart of a modern-day, highly technical America on September 11, 2001. Even at that time, America's interest was more about the gas pump than anything else, but today, we are realizing something even more terrifying. And Marxism has even exerted influence into the Muslim world and formed a culture that can be called Islamo-Marxism.

Since the end of WWII, the last of the Baby Boomers had had been conditioned to avoid socialism and communism. The specter of the Russians taking over the US and the mighty Soviet Union's spreading around the world projected the image of us all being incinerated in a mushroom cloud of global thermonuclear war. We held our collective breath and final exhaled a sigh of relief when the Evil Empire collapsed and disintegrated in 1991. The free world became so ecstatic at that moment to see the enslaved population of the east side of the Berlin Wall begin hammering at that enigmatic barrier that meant the difference between bondage and liberty. That Iron Curtain had crumbled into an elongated mound of rubble to trample over.

This wall actually told a story about two opposing belief systems centering around determining how people were to live. On one side of this wall, there was freedom and liberty, but the other side was a wasteland of human misery with the burning desire to get to the other. As we might know, the city of Berlin is in the nation of Germany. This wall had been constructed by the communist bloc to prevent people from *escaping* to the west. In 1961, as most Berliners were asleep, the city awakened to learn that soldiers had strewn barbed wire to completely separate and dissect the city into two halves. It was as if some gigantic trap had been sprung! Those on the east side of the fence were doomed to stay in the communist domain, and those on the west side of the fence were to live in the democratic side. The barbed wire was eventually replaced with a system of concrete and intermittent barbed wire.

This wall was actually comprised of two parallel concrete walls being about 160 yards apart. Between them was an area of known as a death strip, which was mined with trip wires and patrolled by armed soldiers and guard dogs. Christopher Klein reported, "The 27-mile portion of the barrier separating Berlin into east and west consisted of two concrete walls between which was a 'death strip' up to 160 yards wide that contained hundreds of watchtowers, miles of anti-vehicle trenches, guard dog runs, floodlights, and trip-wire machine guns."[1]

The eastern side of the Berlin Wall, also known as the Iron Curtain, represented the loss of freedom and liberty, while the western side symbolized liberty and the freedom of the human spirit. The

---

[1] Christopher Klein, "10 Things You May Not Know about the Berlin Wall," History, last modified November 9, 2019, https://www.history.com/news/10-things-you-may-not-know-about-the-berlin-wall.

eastern side of the wall had become a prison state where practically every aspect of a person's life was ruled by the government.

But what about socialism after the war in Southeast Asia and the Eastern Bloc of nations that were controlled by Russia? Did we forget about the movement whose ultimate goal was to rule the world? America's time in Vietnam had ended, but the war was still being waged and fought in the minds, if not in the fields of distant lands. As Vietnam reunited, Korea is still divided into North and South, where communism still holds the north and capitalism is the system in the south. Similar to the Berlin Wall, there is an area between the borders that is guarded viciously by the North Koreans—primarily to stop its people from escaping. If you would examine a satellite image of the Korean peninsula at night, you will see a major difference between the two. Notice how bright the lights are in South Korea but note where the darkness starts—at the South and North Korean border! The poverty of North Korea as well as communism in general renders its people into extreme poverty and enslavement, with the exception of those who run the government of course.

There was at the time still the residual effects of the Soviet Union, an ever-increasing power called China began to take its place in spreading the movement throughout the African and South American continents specifically. Communist Cuba, which was basically a boat ride from Florida, has been a prison island since Fidel Castro and his murderous and racist henchman Che Guevara took control of it in 1959. From there, the drive of the human spirit was all but annihilated as the inspiration to excel was diminished into simply the struggle for survival. In Cuba, the average salary for the medical doctor, for example, is only about $225 per month as thousands of citizens cleverly escape every year the Alcatraz-like conditions imposed upon its citizenry.

Some of the African nations had turned their eyes and ears toward the proverbial hammer and sickle to remedy their poverty problems by allowing the military-owned Chinese business machine to come in and conduct, for example, mining operations. Tons of cobalt and lithium are brutally mined—not by machines—but in many cases by children that are practically forced to dig in the pits and tunnels with their bare hands!

Yes, from its inception and the first steps of implementation, the tide of communism has been rising and spreading across the planet—even here in the United States of America—first by the friendly face of the socialism, followed by the absolute brutality of this system itself once the people find themselves irreversibly dependent more upon it than anything else.

We did not even realize the breadth and depth the socialist ideology had extended its branches and dug its roots into America until just recently. After the war in Vietnam, and certainly the collapse of the Soviet Union highlighted the breaking away of those nations which were part of it, America specifically soon forgot about how much of a threat to freedom communism actually was. From that day until now, we had basked in the limelight of believing that our greatest threat to freedom, liberty, and our capitalist system was gone forever.

On the most part, we ignored the struggles of the poor and the rhetoric of academia, unaware that much of what we have seen languishing on our city streets happened to be a predictable outcome. We paid practically no attention to what was being preached and taught in far too many of our churches as Jesus became the unwilling partner with Uncle Sam. As communism began to collapse around the world, academia became the place of sanctuary for its proponents. In fact, just as it was with the Hegels, the Nietzsches, the Darwins, and the Marxes, the world's institutions became the breeding grounds for building a world without God. Perhaps we failed to take seriously the warfare being waged in the spiritual realm, not realizing that they were serious about their efforts to change the world. There is no safer place on earth for the Marxist professors to preach their gospel of anti-capitalist, America-hating philosophies to classroom congregations of students who depended upon and trusted in them. Tenure made them gods! Now its embedded here, but far too many individuals of influence are yet to see socialism's footprints, even as I wrote and you now read. Socialism always puts on a pretty face. It is warm and cuddly, and the life preserver for those who find themselves treading life's deluge of troubles. Socialism pretends to be our savior, making us feel safe and secure—even free from striving to obtain the basic human needs as well as the necessities of life. It even gives the individual the sense of accomplishment at little or no cost because the government is the benevolent giver of all things. This is what it is!

Today, the subtle effects and influences of socialism begins especially within our public-school systems throughout the nation. The programming for redistribution begins there. From the first day of preschool and kindergarten, the child must bring school supplies that were listed on a sheet of paper and posted in stores and supply business for the parents to use when they are out shopping. Does little Johnny or Suzy get to keep those supplies in their desk, locker, or assigned storage area? No! Every student must give the school supplies—the pencils, the crayons, the writing tablets, the scissors, and glue—virtually everything that the parents had purchased according to the list is collected by the teacher and placed in place where all the students will be able to get whatever is needed when or if they either don't have or run out of. This is the beginning of the training for collectivism. Before they are able to read and write, the little tykes are taught a very important lesson on sharing.

We recognize that the human infant's brain needs to be given certain patterns for thinking and reasoning. The first three years of a person's life are extremely important because that is the period in which the human brain is in essence, programmed. Very precious, but significant moments and events help determine so much in the child that affects them for the rest of their lives. Personality traits are formed. The way they learn is established and certain behaviors are instilled and reinforced, including in many cases, collectivism. Once that groove is cut, it is practically impossible to perform any other way unless to program crashes, and the system is erased or wiped clean. Then reprogramming is possible. In a sense, it is very comparable to programming a computer or, more accurately, a computer disk. In either case, the equipment must be programmed in order for it to operate correctly. It must be capable of performing many and various tasks, such as simply starting up when the power button is pressed and presenting various items and applications on what is known as the desktop.

So in consideration of this child, imagine what can happen to this tiny toddler who is sent to a preschool-aged program, where collectivism is a key component in their preparation for entry into the public education system. "We must teach our children about the virtues of sharing" is a common explanation. "We want to make certain that those who cannot afford school supplies does not get embarrassed in front of those who can" is another. Common ownership of property and redistribution of goods seem to be noble causes to teach three to five-year-olds, but the programming can last a lifetime unless redirected towards a more fulfilling purpose such as, for example, Christianity.

Then picture that same individual as a millennial years later at their high school graduation exercise, receiving that much sought-after diploma. "In fact, according to the report, 60 percent of millennials (age 24–39) support a 'complete change of our economic system away from capitalism,' and 57 percent of Gen Z does as well: increases of 8 and 14 percentage points, respectively, from just last year."[2] Could this be a determining factor that has influenced so many young adults? Additionally, in referring again to the group of millennials in America, about 20 percent of them believe that the holocaust—the deliberate extermination of over six million Jews—never happened. These issues reflect the direction that our public education system has been going. This is not error but intentional.

John M. Ellis, author of *The Breakdown of Higher Education*, wrote a commentary in the *Wall Street Journal*, titled "Higher Ed Has Become a Threat to America,"[3] which is about how devastating the academic culture in America has been to the generations at least since World War II. He writes:

---

[2] David Fitzgerald and Gabriel Black, "Support for Socialism Jumps by Nearly 10 Percent among US Youth amid Pandemic Depression," World Socialist Web Site, October 22, 2020, https://www.wsws.org/en/articles/2020/10/23/soci-o23.html.

[3] *Wall Street Journal*, Opinion Section, December 4, 2023.

Children's test scores have plummeted because college education departments train teachers to prioritize "social justice" over education. Censorship started with one-party campuses shutting down conservative voices. The coddling of criminals originated with academia's devotion to Michel Foucault's idea that criminals are victims, not victimizers. The drive to separate children from their parents begins in long-standing campus contempt for the suburban home and nuclear family. Radicalized college journalism departments promote far-left advocacy. Open borders reflect pro-globalism and anti-nation state sentiment among radical professors. DEI started as a campus ruse to justify racial quotas. Campus antisemitism grew out of ideologies like "anticolonialism," "anticapitalism" and "intersectionality."

Another issue to seriously examine is based upon the fallacy that there is an infinite barrel of cash that finances every issue and program imposed upon this nation in the effort to exercise benevolence, but the real goal is to destroy America as we know it today. When our agencies and departments are being overwhelmed with unimaginable numbers of social services in particular, recognize that these events and situations are neither accidental nor coincidental—they are intentional.

Perhaps you have not ever heard of the Cloward-Piven Strategy. Richard Cloward and wife Frances Fox Piven were sociologists at Columbia University during the sixties. After observing the 1965 riots in the Watts district of Los Angeles, California, they were inspired to develop a strategy for destroying capitalism by "overloading the system," especially in the area of welfare and social services. At a minimum, they were socialists and were very instrumental in creating the "crisis strategy." Cloward and Piven published an article titled, "The Weight of the Poor: A Strategy to End Poverty," in the

May 2, 1966, issue of *The Nation*. Following its publication, *The Nation* sold an unprecedented thirty thousand reprints.[4]

There will be instances where you will probably seek to find some logical reason people treat others in such cruel ways, and why some people seek to live in ways that simply don't make much sense. Hopefully, you will consider what the Cloward-Piven Strategy is intended to do: make the system so overburdened in its efforts to actually *help* people that it collapses beneath the burden of its own intentions. Homelessness, mobs ransacking high-end department and jewelry stores, gun violence, fentanyl and millions of illegal immigrants flooding our borders while our cities are straining practically every aspect of our way of life. In these times when things do not make much sense, at least consider the possibility that they may just be intentional.

This book presents a series of eight relatively short lessons concerning the basic ideology of socialism and the hidden dangers lurking just below the calm waves of deceit. In short, socialism is man's attempt to create a perfect, utopian world without the presence or acknowledgement of God. The entire system is built upon the principle of collectivist thinking and planning by a group and subgroups of elitists, who design and plan their entire lives for all else. Please use these lessons to promote education and conversation—especially with the unwary.

I must confess that I am a Christian and am compelled to see things from this perspective; however, I would be embarrassingly negligent if I were to intentionally exclude any references or mention of my God, the Bible, or some of the scriptural expressions of the people of faith as well as of those who contributed to the founding of this great nation as well as those who came after them but contributed to its betterment. Our faith is kind and tolerable of other belief systems but will be unapologetically determined to resist anything or anyone who seeks to dismantle the Judeo-Christian foundations as Marxism intends. Socialism is a strong attraction for individuals

---

[4] Richard Poe, Discover the Networks, 2005, https://www.discoverthenetworks.org/.

of all faiths, cultures, and beliefs but is determined to destroy these foundational principles as it has done in other nations. This secular world may teach that it is better to free oneself from the drudgery and dictatorial burdens of being obligated to an invisible deity and live a life where all things are provided by a collective of fellow *believers*. It imitates the goodness of the Christian faith and presents itself as the best way to live as well as caring for this world, but be warned: socialism and its older brother communism have a built-in kill switch that activates when the populace comes to the point of realizing that they cannot live in a controlled system, and are willing to even fight for the freedom they (or their ancestors) had lost. The human spirit can only be contained or subdued for so long.

A final and very important note: even Karl Marx acknowledged that socialism is the transitional social state between the overthrow of capitalism and the realism of communism. He is credited with being the great creator of both socialism and communism. This is the most likely reason the term *Marxism* is more common than the mention of Hegelian (Georg Friedrich) or Engelsism (Frederick), the two most influential philosophers of Marx's focus of study. Though none of these and most other contributors to the atheistic view of the world, it was Russia's Joseph Stalin who applied their theories into the practical rule of people through the force of government. Although the name of Karl Marx or Marxism may be often mentioned, this primer is not intended to spend much time discussing his life nor the lives of others and how he figures into our modern world.

For these and other reasons, *Understanding Socialism_*is here hopefully in due season to help challenge socialism's hidden traps for bondage and prayerfully turn this encroachment upon the freedoms we have enjoyed and shared for generations into a system that our post-Vietnam generations to reject it as we had done. Welcome to Socialism 101!

SOCIALISM REJECTS GOD

I wish myself against the One who rules above. I will
wander godlike and victorious through the ruins of
this world. This haven't I forfeited. I know it full well.
My soul, once true to God is chosen for hell.

—Karl Marx

Most of us probably have not paid much attention—if any
at all—to the number of individuals today who use much of their
wealth to reshape, reform or as some popularly say, reimagine the
world and things to be different from the way they are today. The
vast number probably would like to impact a part of the world with
the intention of to make it better. But what if making it better meant
using the resources they had meant for creating a utopian society or

world? There are very wealthy individuals—billionaires in particular—who work feverishly to do just that. Individuals like George Soros, Bill Gates, Mark Zuckerberg, Jeff Bezos, and Elon Musk are to name a few. According to Einar H. Divyk, a researcher at an organization named Statista and to our surprise, there are more billionaires in communist China than there are in the free world like the United States. Mr. Divyk, who monitors economy, politics, and society from a global perspective,[5] observes that in the year 2023 China had 969 billionaires and the United States had 691. On the other hand, John Hyatt of Forbes says that America has 735 billionaires while China has 495.

But the question of what will they use their wealth for has more significance than how much money they might have. How will they use their wealth, should they choose to do so, to influence and affect the culture? As we know, George Soros has used a significant amount of his wealth to help left-leaning district attorneys and judges to be elected to political office—especially to influence our major cities. Zuckerberg has contributed hundreds of millions to support voter access to ballot boxes. What if there is a concerted effort to establish a form of globalized socialism or much worse, communism. What if the billionaires of China, the United States and other nations lock arms and focus on establishing some type of global unity?

During the days of September 3–6, 2012, the Democrat Party held its national convention in Charlotte, North Carolina. Among other issues, this four-day event was also highlighted by what had happened as the party's National Committee had radically changed the party's platform as well as removing the typical invocations and references to God and God-given rights. They had also purposefully removed the language that affirmed Jerusalem as being the capital of the nation Israel. One might ask, "Why would someone seek to do such a thing?" When many of the delegates learned of this bold but callous move, they were outraged and insisted that the wording be restored back into the national platform.

---

[5] https://www.statista.com/aboutus/our-research-commitment/3018/einar-h-dyvik

On Wednesday, September 5, there arose an uproar that was led by former Ohio governor Ted Strickland, who spoke from the convention's center podium. The tension in that convention was clearly discernable in the atmosphere. It was obvious, as thick as cigar smoke in a beer joint—nearly suffocating in the public air. Who would want to stand in the midst of the heaviness of the spiritual battle being waged between the pro-God faction and the anti-God faction? It was certainly an unenviable moment as Governor Strickland came to the microphone to speak.

> This summer I was proud to serve this party as the platform drafting committee chair. As the chair, I come before you today to discuss two important matters related to our party's national platform. As an ordained United Methodist minister, I am here to attest and affirm that our faith and belief in God is central to the American story, and informs the values we expressed in our party's platform. In addition, President Obama recognizes Jerusalem as the capital of Israel, and our party's platform should as well.
>
> Mr. Chairman, I have submitted my amendment in writing and I believe it is being projected on the screen for the delegates to see. I move adoption of the amendment as submitted and shown to the delegates.

After introducing an amendment to restore the omitted language back into the party's platform, convention chairman Antonio Villaraigosa, then Los Angeles mayor, put the amendment to a voice vote on the convention floor, requiring a two-thirds majority for passage. This method was obviously doomed from the start. Perhaps Villaraigosa and the convention coordinators thought that this exercise would be open-and-shut event, just a momentary distraction, but the entire session was turned into a donnybrook of opposing forces. At least it may have been loud and vocal, but no violence.

Then Los Angeles mayor Antonio Villaraigosa presided over the most embarrassing moments in Democratic Party history: voting to reject God.

After the first vote was judged to have been indecisive because of the seemingly equal volume of voices, a stunned Villaraigosa called for a second vote, which was again met with an equal volume of ayes and nos. A female convention official who was standing beside him to his left whispered advisedly, "You've got to rule, and then you've got to let them do what they're gonna do."

Villaraigosa embarrassingly then called a third vote with the same result. By that time, he was past being able to call right wrong, and the entire world witnessed the lie! At the end of the third attempt to correct this boondoggle by voice vote, Chairman Villaraigosa then sheepishly declared that the amendment had passed by the majority voice vote, causing an eruption of boos on the floor—even louder than the vote itself. From the *at-home* television view, anyone could see how embarrassingly awkward that moment was. We could see the absolute fear in his eyes. Chairman Villaraigosa had lied.

Perhaps a decibel meter to measure the loudness generated by each group, but the nos seemingly were louder. Without a doubt, an objective vote by actual ballot would have made the decision without question but also exposed the party for its real and true intentions—

to remove God and his word from their hopes and dreams. One thing was certain, the mere thought of rejecting any references to God was an earth-moving event itself. There are many Christians who associate themselves and identify as being members of the Democrat Party, but it is doubtful that they are aware of this occurrence even today. But the question still unanswered has been, "Why did the leaders of the Democrat Party, this once-revered political organization, seek to remove any and everything in reference to God from their national platform?" Perhaps it was because God was in the way. It would be impossible for them to do the things they wanted to do with, for, or, most likely, *to* America itself—create one nation *without* God!

Governor Strickland and other convention delegates were obviously Christians determined to preserve the last remaining parts of the traditional Democrat Party. Apparently, they had been blind-sided by what the national committee had attempted to do. Has anyone ever asked, "Why?" It is commendable for the governor, and his supporters stood up and made their voices heard, but if you were to listen to the voice vote in the facility, most people believe that the highly motivated delegates who wanted to remove the references were actually louder. It was also plain to see that the former mayor was extremely embarrassed. He appeared to have been paralyzed with fear instead of showing confidence in what he had just presided over. Should Christians be confident in their future efforts?

Devoid of divine influences, socialism's essence is based upon man's intellect and wisdom. For its proponents and practitioners to function well and effectively, God is not necessary. In fact, God is the hindrance, and the notion of being a part his kingdom is repulsive! The socialist system demands that he must be replaced above all else because atheism is the system that lays the foundation for doing just that! So the Democrat Party's National Convention in Charlotte was the work of one of America's two major political organizations, representing at least 80 million registered voters that sought to divorce itself from any relationship with God.

Simply put, this system is based upon the human effort to create a perfect, utopian world without the need for nor belief in God of the Bible. This is why Marxist-leaning politicians first offer certain goods and services—usually promises they either cannot or do not intend to keep. Socialism is constantly seeking to endear itself within the hearts of people primarily by posing as the benevolent source for all things, with this purpose expressed through the power of government. Unfortunately, the Democrat Party convention's governing committee and many of the delegates that convened in Charlotte, North Carolina, during that week of September of 2012 sought to do just that!

In other words, this system, driven by individuals who have no fundamental belief in God seeks a society and world order based upon the power and intellect of a collective humanity. For them, Christianity itself is the ultimate obstacle. Not only is there a lack of the belief in a higher being, but these individuals also seek greatness through the exercising of governmental power and authority, rewarding the faithful and punishing the dissenters.

This also explains why Christianity is so hated and increasingly vilified in this world today because Jesus himself makes it plainly understood about his uniqueness in this creation. In John 14:6, Jesus proclaimed, "I am the way, the truth, and the life: no man cometh unto the Father, but by me."

> ... politics is the battlefield by which the spiritual warfare of our day is being waged. For us to withdraw is to surrender.

Socialism cannot be successful if the people believe in the One True Living God of the Bible, or quite possibly other belief systems that may place emphasis upon individual liberty or place focus upon a deity that claims a uniqueness that rivals the socialist model as Christianity does. Those who believe in a secular system usually are irritated by those expressing true faith and devotion to the Savior and our Heavenly Father and will become increasingly angry and antagonistic as according to biblical teachings and prophesy the evil days come nearer. So let us pray for those who are falling prey to this great deception.

> But if our gospel be hid, it is hid to them that are lost. In whom the god of this world hath blinded the minds of them which believe not, lest the light of the glorious gospel of Christ, who is the image of God, should shine unto them. (2 Corinthians 4:3–4).

Of any of the architects who plan this and other forms of social engineering, not one of them would dare base their positions on God or his word, or they thought they wouldn't. They are the ones most likely vehemently protest any attempt to associate religion with politics in any manner, but the political realm is where they themselves feverishly fight to eliminate every aspect of it from the public square if not the human heart altogether. Separation of church and state is the mantra blurted out without thought. However, those of religious conviction not only should involve themselves, but must! Why? Because politics is the battlefield by which the spiritual warfare of our day is being waged. For us to withdraw is to surrender.

Socialism's very nature itself consists of the rejection of God or any deity that a population may worship because those people must be placed in the state of dependency upon the governing system—a form of bondage. The socialist facilitator seeks to establish a form of governance and control that places them into the seat of unquestionable power that cannot be challenged. Even their perspective of the universe is that the creation is a product of evolution and chance. No intelligent being (God) exists nor ever existed according to Darwin's book. This means that man himself is the ultimate source of wisdom and power because it is he, and only he is the most advanced being in existence (as according to the evolutionary scale or ladder). He is God. There is no being other than him.

Man is the ultimate entity—the period at the end of the book of evolutionary ascendency that tells the narrative of humanity's multibillion-year journey from the primordial concoction of chemicals through the single-celled organism phase and on up through the plant and animal kingdom to his state of existence today. For the socialist mindset, there was no intelligent designer, planner, and much less a creator. There was no cosmic maestro there to conduct the movements of the great orchestra of stars and planets in the universe. Man sees himself as being the sum total of all that crept up from the Great Ooze of Probability; and therefore, it is man who stands as the ultimate of all living things—he is God! His vision of evolutionary ascendency will enable him to one day rise above the stars to claim his ultimate dominion with the ability to determine which stars to turn on and which ones to extinguish. He will be the creator of worlds!

Finally, we can define and discuss the meanings of socialism and communism from the academic perspective, elaborating on the relationship between those who wield the power and influence that controls the means of production and how it is done. But on the other hand, I would prefer to speak of these two terms from a very practical point of view. Socialism is when the people *believe* that government is god, and communism is when government *becomes* god. As Marx saw it, socialism is the halfway point between capitalism and communism. When the people *enjoy* the benefits of the socialist culture, this time period can be seen as the courtship phase. The leaders of the plan work to make life for the targeted group as easy as possible.

Even here in the United States of America, certain cities are experimenting with *minimum basic income* where families are given a monthly sum of money just for being a resident. There are little or no requirements, and the monthly stipends may range from five hundred dollars to one thousand dollars. Like the crack cocaine dealer offering the future addict the first crack rock, the socialists within our US federal government have also been eagerly planning to do its part to establish this system of dependency nationwide. "If you become a recipient of the minimum basic income program, you don't have to worry about a job. You can go and do whatever your heart desires—become an artist, learn to play a musical instrument, travel." This is the courtship period. It is timeless, lasting as long as the system can support its citizenry, but when it becomes incapable, the courtship ends.

Let us recall President Lyndon B. Johnson's so-called War on Poverty. It was allegedly meant to boost the poorest families in America with cash and food. In his book *A Dream Derailed: How the Left Hijacked Civil Rights to Create A Permanent Underclass*, Reverend Bill Owens documents the path to controlled poverty that President Lyndon B. Johnson's War on Poverty created. A veteran warrior of the civil rights era, Rev. Owens lived and experienced practically every aspect of life as a young black man in the hostile South. He fellowshipped and marched with Rev. Dr. Martin Luther King and other leaders at the tip of the spear in the movement, but there was president Johnson's strategic plan that all but nullified the movement that was immortalized in King's *I Have A Dream* speech. Instead, a large part of the black population became engulfed in the welfare state. Rev. Owens explains the situation as such:

> President Lyndon Johnson enacted the food stamp program in 1964 as part of the Great Society plan… When Congress created food stamps, thousands of welfare recruiters were sent into cities across the nation to sign up low-income mothers for government welfare and food stamps. *In Liberal Fascism,*[6] Jonah Goldberg wrote about targeted nature of this campaign: "James Bovard notes that when Congress mandated food stamps, welfare 'recruiters'—a hundred thousand of them created by the War On Poverty—went into the cities to convince poor people to enroll."[7]

---

[6] Jonah Goldberg, *Liberal Fascism: The History of the American Left, from Mussolini to the Politics Change*; New York: Broadway Books, 2007.

[7] Rev. Bill and Deborah Owens, *A Dream Derailed: How the Left Hijacked Civil Rights to Create A Permanent Underclass*; A New Dream Publishers, 2019.

The War on Poverty was actually controlled behavior modification—a form of experimentation in socialism. The black community became the petri dish for learning methods in manipulating mass populations. Temporary support became generational dependency.

> Government dependency helped create the issues in black America that we see today. Untold thousands of single mothers with multiple children—many from different fathers, and all on welfare—are raising their children without fathers in the home… Black men, who once worked to support their families and provided authority and stability in their homes, are no longer around serving as role models for our black sons… As more young boys grew up without fathers, they lacked the foundation fathers provide. Many have turned to life in the streets with gangs, drugs and crime—looking for the guidance and authority that a father provides.[8]

Historically, some countries have embraced some form of socialism for decades. For example, the French Revolution of 1789 was highlighted by the guillotine. Rebelling from the aristocracy and Christianity itself, the rebels executed the royalty, the wealthy, and the clergy to become a nation officially free of religion.

Remember the Cloward-Piven Strategy mentioned earlier? It is just as effective anywhere in the world as it is in America. If or when the government is no longer able to afford to continue supplying said provisions to the people, they become unhappy as we see happening in France today. Having become used to and dependent upon those provisions, there will be marches, acts of violence, and other forms of protests. In Venezuela, Hugo Chavez obtained the presidency of the country by promising "the easy life" for everybody. This nation's infrastructure tells of a time not too long ago where its citizens were

---

[8] Ibid.

living a relatively high standard of living with a very strong middle class. To place Venezuela in the proper perspective, it is a founding member of the Organization of Petroleum Exporting Countries, otherwise known as OPEC. Its citizenry boasted of the prestige of being part of the oil producing nations as they benefitted from the revenue.

Chavez's Venezuelan utopia soon began to collapse because it takes high concentrations of revenue to satisfy the people's needs, and the courtship began to turn into something different.

Throughout his first term, Chavez's plans to reform policies in keeping with his leftist ideology faltered. Although he enjoyed the support of the working class for his spending on education, food coupons, and social services, other Venezuelans opposed his programs[9], and in 2001, the implementation of his economic reforms prompted massive protests and strikes.[10] His government soon realized that there was not enough revenue generating to keep the promises he had made. Tax increases and the rationing of goods and services became the catalyst for social unrest. Once a hero, President Chavez soon became the face of distrust for the very people who once supported him—especially the university student population. "Interior Ministry, spray them with gas and dissolve any disturbance. We cannot begin showing weakness as a government," Chavez said during a campaign meeting at a historic Venezuelan battleground.

Utopia is extremely expensive where every nation or society has tried it eventually fails with the loss of life and extensive destruction. After Chavez's death due to cancer, his lieutenant and strongman Nicholas Maduro took over the nation as president, unleashing a tide of brutality against dissenters and protestors. According to the United States Department of State report on the brutality imposed upon the Venezuelan people by the illegitimate Maduro regime:

- In October 2018, Caracas Councilman Fernando Alban traveled to New York to denounce the Maduro regime's

---

[9] Reuters Staff, "Venezuela's Chavez Urges Tear Gas against Protests," last modified January 19, 2009, https://www.reuters.com/article/venezuela-chavez-idUSN1731625820090118.

[10] "The Hugo Chavez Presidency," Britannica, https://www.britannica.com/place/Venezuela/The-Hugo-Chavez-presidency.

brutality on the sidelines of the United Nations General Assembly. Upon his return to Venezuela on October 5, Maduro's secret police arrested him at the airport. He died in custody a few days later when he mysteriously fell from a tenth-floor window of a maximum-security prison in Caracas.

- Maduro has increasingly relied on the Special Action Force of the National Police (FAES) that he created in 2017 to carry out illegal raids and extrajudicial killings.
- The FAES, comprised of 1,300 officers, stands accused of killing more than one hundred people in low-income neighborhoods from June to December 2018. (January 26, 2019, NGO Provea report)[11]
- On March 20, 2019, according to the UN High Commissioner for Human Rights Michelle Bachelet, FAES executed thirty-seven people in connection with illegal home-invasion raids in January.

Stories and reports of human desperation were many as even the grocery stores, supermarkets, and farms became barren and desolate partly from the lack of supply and partly because of unqualified and incompetent government bureaucrats placed into position because of political affiliation instead of real knowledge and qualification. Homes, stores, warehouses, and other sources of food were literally stripped and ravaged of any and every morsel of food. Wild birds and animals began to disappear. From the stores to private property. Reports of stolen pets from the yards and aquariums at homes, animal care facilities, and even zoos reflected how desperate the once-thriving people of Venezuela had become under the Chavez-Maduro regimes. The promise had become a fatalistic deception. Socialistic promises sound good but always fail.

This great OPEC nation, a favorite vacation spot for the world's jetsetters, a nation filled with some of the world's most generous and

---

[11] "January 26, 2019, NGO Provea Report," US Department of State, Office of the Spokesperson—US Secretary of State Mike Pompeo, March 19, 2019.

hardworking people, was turned into a third-world dictatorship within a period of a few years. It was transformed from being the envy of the South American continent into a poverty-stricken hellhole to escape from!

This is the typical cycle of bondage and dictatorial enslavement of a nation that goes from freedom to dependency to enslavement. Venezuela's socialist experiment began with the Chavez courtship that included the proverbial wining-and-dining period. Promises were made that everyone would be taken care of—all the physical needs would be free and readily available. Those who had much became the enemies of those who had little or nothing—it was the wealthy people's fault that the other people were poor. This convinced the majority of the Venezuelan population—or at least those who voted for Hugo Chavez—to abandon the basic system of capitalistic enterprise and personal accountability in favor of cradle-to-grave care by the government.

People who receive free stuff will always seek one thing—*more* free stuff. The Venezuelan system became overloaded to the point that it could not afford the monetary burden placed upon it by the demands of the people who expected the promises be kept. Then came the cutbacks in services, bankruptcies and inflation, and many other issues, including unemployment. The protesters marched in the streets against government's failure to keep their promises, only curtailed by antiprotester gangs and government agencies. This brought out the military, led by a brutal leader determined to eliminate all opposition. Thus, Venezuela has cycled from freedom to dependency to bondage that culminates with brutal and murderous President Maduro. According to a CBS News report, as many as fifty thousand Venezuelans illegally entered the U.S. through the southern border during September of 2023 alone![12]

Venezuela is not the only example of what happens when men seek to provide the needs of a population through government force

---

[12] Camilo Montoya-Galvez, CBS News: "Record number of Venezuelan migrants crossed U.S.-Mexico border in September, internal data show," October 4, 2023

without reference to nor belief in God-—humanity's eternal hope and inspiration. Socialism can only carry a man so far because of its own limitation: revenue. Neither can it revive the spirit nor replenish the soul. Like its elder brother, communism, socialism envies God because it wants to be God; not necessarily in the form of a person, but one of certain attributes such as having the power to provide, produce, and rule.

SOCIALISM'S MORALITY IS BUILT UPON MAN'S SENSE OF RIGHT AND WRONG

When the material world came into existence, it was based upon the rule and control of certain laws and principles that are true. Not only that, but these principles are also predictable, and when violated by the things which are subject to them are destined to be destroyed or transformed into something else. For example, physics is a science that covers numerous areas governed by certain properties and principles in nature surrounding matter and energy. Matter itself can never be destroyed but is changed from one form to another and the same principle applies to energy. Neither can it be destroyed. These are the basic laws of chemistry.

When it comes to science, principles govern the material world.

Last of all, there is what we generally know as morality. Notice that this principle does not apply to nature—we do not say it's immoral or sinful for a large tree to be blown by a strong wind, causing it to fall on your house. Neither do we consider it to be sinful for a dog to bite a person on the leg. Many times we experience, or at least hear about, devastating weather such as tornados, hurricanes, or catastrophic floods, but we never associate such events with morality. However, when we look at morality first as being one of the universe's viable principles that is just as significant as physics, or any other principle, we cannot help but to acknowledge what it means and what (or who) it governs. To bring this point home, morality exists to govern the behavior of both men and angels! In this case, who would you trust to establish these principles, man or God?

However, there may be an issue of morality if there was a person involved who knew that that tree was leaning in a way in which, if it were to fall, the house would be in its path of falling—the direction by which the home would be totally crushed and destroyed. And if that person were to take a chainsaw and cut that tree so that it would destroy the house, there the question of morality comes into play. Similarly, there would be a moral question if there was a person who commanded that dog to attack the individual. Morality applies to the behavior and conduct of human beings and angels, creatures that have free wills with the ability to make choices. Most importantly, the question of where humanity gets his morals from suggests that they have to derive from a source greater than and outside of the realm of humanity itself!

In Russian novelist Fyodor Dostoevsky's *The Brothers Karamazov*, Dmitri Karamazov famously poses the question of what would happen to mankind without some form of defining order. The key thought interjected is "If God is dead, then everything is permitted." In other words, the laws of God have proven themselves in providing and establishing a foundation of living for each person, a community, and even a nation. If there is no God, then someone has to set universal values and standards that govern the human population. But what does morality mean? First of all, the *American Heritage Dictionary* defines the term as "the quality of being in accord with standards of right or good conduct" or "a system of ideas of right and wrong conduct."[13]

Secondly, the following definitions encourage additional exploration of morality's meaning because this word is so important in this nation and more so for this world! The excerpt comes from an online site that hopefully inspires us seek a deeper and become more appreciative of what morality really means:

> Principles concerning the distinction between
> right and wrong or good and bad behavior; a par-

---

[13] *The American Heritage Dictionary* (Boston: Houghton Mifflin Company, 1985).

ticular system of values and principles of conduct, especially one held by a specified person or society; the extent to which an action is right or wrong.[14]

Humanity cannot exist in chaos because the human brain itself must be given the opportunity to make rational order of the material world, especially within its immediate surroundings and environment. While the healthy brain seeks to bring order and rational thought, it takes the principles available and formulates a world that is universally beneficial for itself as well as everyone else. Its world becomes comprehensive as well as productive. On the other hand, the unhealthy or damaged brain is usually steeped in disorder and confusion as well as an unawareness of those things we consider. But what happens when the healthy brain is exposed to principles that are not universally beneficial but destructive? It is God who first introduced the notion of good and evil. It was he who warned Adam and Eve of the consequences of embracing those principles that would lead to destruction, including death itself!

Who determines what the principles are? Who values or weighs the content of each meaning? If God or at least some all-powerful deity doesn't, who wields the power, wisdom, and flawless intellectualism? Without transcendent and universal codes for behavior that enables all men the opportunity to adapt to the world's conditions, as well as navigate through the sea of humanity without hindrance and interference is ideal, but there actually are not any that are devised by men because their goals are normally driven to dominate and control. He has imagined into *existence* gods he chose to serve with his heart, mind, and soul, but they were merely tragic and often brutal extensions of his own psyche. This brings us to the point of what socialism requires of its adherents.

Above all things, socialism is based upon the human effort to create a perfect, utopian world without the need for or belief in God, completely equipped with its bible of moral principles borrowed from philosophical works such as Karl Marx's *The Communist Manifesto.*

---

[14] Oxford Languages, 2023, https://languages.oup.com/google-dictionary-en/.

Employing principles laid forth from atheists such as Marx, socialism is constantly seeking to endear itself within the hearts of people primarily by posing as a benevolent source for all things, with this purpose initially introduced through the power of government provisions ranging from food to salvation. In other words, this system, driven by individuals who have no fundamental belief in God seek a world order based upon the power and intellect of people deemed superior. These "gods" are the guardians, the producers, and the sources for all that is determined to be right and wrong.

To the Germans, Adolf Hitler was a god. In Russia, and eventually the Soviet Union, Vladimir Lenin and Joseph Stalin were gods. In China, Chairman Mao Zedong became the unquestionable god before the people. In Cuba, the school system used ice cream to convince the youth that Fidel Castro was more dependable than God. In North Korea, the formidable statues and images of founder Kim Il Sung and his son Kim Jong Il and now Kim Jong Il impose terror and fear throughout the population because in their minds, they are gods!

To expel the old, especially the people's way of thinking and even their language itself had to be altered. The definition of words must be changed in order to manipulate and transform the thinking of the people. Good easily becomes evil and the evil quickly becomes good when the people are starving.

Because all natural laws and moral principles of the universe come from the God of Creation, anything outside of his moral law is false, meaning that man's establishment of his own concept of morality are therefore fallible and subject to the dictates of those in power. When man rejects God, he then develops a code of behavior to govern himself and others, usually with a small elite group being exempt from the very laws they impose upon the governed. We have learned through history that the laws and principles created by humanity are never stable nor dependable. This small elite group become the gods of this world. They become the champions of the poor and protectors of the ones who are actually the victims of the very laws they implement and enforce. This is what dependency is all about.

The elites use their morality to create circumstances that grant them even more power and use it to punish or even eliminate those who may dissent or disagree. Throughout history, man's morality has justified the slaughter of over 100 million innocent souls for the purpose of accomplishing their own visions. For example, some believe (and fear) that the earth is already overpopulated by many who are quickly consuming the planet's natural resources. The moral thing for them is to "decrease the population by any means necessary."

There have been those who believed (and still do!) that their particular race was destined to evolve into a super-superior class with godlike qualities. Thus, it was their moral duty to accelerate this process by ridding the world of what they saw as "inferior" races under the animal kingdom's survival of the fittest dogma. Another ideology says that humanity is the cause for the earth's rising (and falling) temperatures. Therefore, there must be a set of rules, standards, and principles that must be employed and followed for the purpose of saving the planet—including forcing the earth's citizenry to rid themselves of carbon dioxide generating gases.

> For they being ignorant of God's righteousness, and going about to establish their own righteousness, have not submitted themselves unto the righteousness of God. (Romans 10:3)

Can you trust man's morality? Has he demonstrated that his guidelines are sufficient? Would his morality be universally applied to all men for all time? Consider the question from this perspective—if we do not have a creator, then we are what the evolutionists say we are, simply bundles of chemical reactions and microelectric impulses that have evolved from a primordial soup. Man would then be the originator and deliverer of right and wrong, good and evil. He would have to also be the enforcer of these principles, but his principles would be subject to change.

Much of our culture today believe this, and one of its disciplines is known as secular humanism. This belief system focuses on the way human beings can lead happy and functional lives. It posits that human beings are capable of being ethical and moral without religion or God; it neither assumes humans to be inherently evil or innately good, nor presents humans as above nature or superior to it.

SOCIALISM IS FALSE CHRISTIANITY

Rev. Jim Jones was the founder and leader of the People's Temple Cult and used Christianity to push communism. Source: Wikipedia

Imagine a world in which every person was treated exactly the same. Each individual being provided food, clothing, and shelter as well as the consistent preaching that promote the ideas of how great their system is, but those who are not part of it are missing out on the system's goodness. You are *taken care of* from cradle to grave. You are encouraged to not ever worry nor be concerned about your provisions because this system is fully capable of supplying each and every one of your needs—all your material and psychological (spiritual) necessities to ensure your happiness and personal and social fulfillment. This is heaven on earth. This is utopia!

In this utopian society, there is no racism, no homophobia, no xenophobia, nor any other phobia or form of hatred or rejection.

Being tightly and smugly cocooned in guaranteed security, this system ensures that there is no need to feel lost or destitute. There is no need to fear fellow believers for the enemy—this devil is not part of this culture because all dissention and resistance is from without. Salvation is not the gifted act of some almighty being in the cosmos; it is all planned and designed exclusively by great and intelligent people—charismatics, philosophers, and academics to name a few. But the almighty power to ensure these blessings are made available through the government. The *Columbia Encyclopedia* defines government as "a system of social control under which the right to make laws, and the right to enforce them, is vested in a particular group in society."

It is most likely that you have heard the expression, "Don't drink the Kool-Aid!" However, it is doubtful that the majority of those born after 1980 would have any knowledge of where this phrase came from. Neither would they know about the Jonestown, Guyana, tragedy, the People's Temple cult, and the founder of it all—the Indiana-born preacher who caused over nine hundred people to die either by committing suicide, being murdered because they refused to follow Reverend Jones's orders, or by being injected with the cyanide-based by syringe because they were too young to do it themselves.

At the pinnacle of his diabolical work, the Rev. Jim Jones had become the envy of preachers, politicians, and professionals, to name a few categories of people. Hollywood was fascinated with him as many of the movie stars and TV personalities attended his services. Throughout the early to midseventies, Reverend Jones was the "king maker" in California politics, especially within the Democrat Party. It was said that if a person wanted to run for a political office in California, they would have to get the approval of Rev. Jim Jones.

> If you're born in capitalist America, racist America, fascist America, then you're born in sin. But if you're born in socialism, you're not born in sin. (Rev. Jim Jones)

But the key point to make is extremely important. the deviously evil work of Rev. Jim Jones, though deceptive was the envy of a significant part of the Christian community—especially in California. Reverend Jones and his closest followers staged many faith healing events. He preached his full gospel and Pentecostal sermons to the general public, but at home in the People's Temple facilities, his messages were not about the Kingdom of God.

> Man, the only sin's you're born in, is the society, the kind of community you live in. If you're born in a socialist community, then you're not born in sin. (Pause) If you're born in this church, this socialist revolution, you're not born in born in sin. If you're born in capitalist America, racist America, fascist America, then you're born in sin. But if you're born in socialism, you're not born in sin. (Rev. Jim Jones)[15]

Obviously, the People's Temple cult and its leader, Rev. Jim Jones, bore the appearance of many facets of the Christian faith and some of its exercises of faith, but he certainly was preparing his followers and members to embrace socialism. They were actually being brainwashed—literally brainwashed to death! Up to that point, this cult appeared to have been a group of believers in Jesus Christ, led by a charismatic preacher. This organization carried a thin veneer of Christianity, with a deep foundation of Marxist socialism! Clear evidence that socialism easily imitates Christianity but obviously false. Socialism is false Christianity!

Politicians such as Governor Edmund Brown and son Jerry, state assemblyman and eventual San Francisco mayor Willie Brown, Diane Feinstein, Barbara Boxer, and Nancy Pelosi, and many other Californians were in partnership with Reverend Jones. In addition, Washington DC elites such as First Lady Roslyn Carter and Vice

---

[15] Fielding M. McGehee III, "Q1053-4 Transcript," Jonestown Institute, last modified July 10, 2023, https://jonestown.sdsu.edu/?page_id=27318.

President Walter Mondale flew to California to privately (secretly) meet with him.

However, as with the Reverend Jones, we find that the basic plot bears no difference with the poor victims of Jonestown, Guyana, and the group of people who seek to establish this lifestyle as the basic pattern for human living. It may benefit a few but is devastating for the vast majority of the population it involves. Those who benefit are the ones who still remain attached to their own personal drive that employs the use of their own gifts, talents, and intellect to rise above the norm and soar above the status quo. Unfortunately, these successful ones become the scorn of the majority as individualism is the cardinal sin above all else. The few who actually benefit from this system become the leaders, the rulers, and the key movers and shakers. They become the decision-makers while the great multitude become dependent on them. This is socialism at its best!

The lore of living in a perfect world has been the passion of men from the very beginning of recorded history. No more worries, no more sadness, no more sickness, no more pain or poverty. You can live in an environment similar to the way (believe it or not), that Adam and Eve lived in that perfect place called the Garden of Eden.

Christianity does not present itself solely as the way to navigate through life in this physical world but offers a plan of preparation for the life to come, which we call *eternity* or the state of existence where time is no longer applicable. From the theological perspective, eternity means endless life after death in this world. Death does not mean the cessation of consciousness and existence—it means separation. The Christian view tells us that humanity, as well as the material world, is destined to exist well beyond the current state of being.

In comparison, socialism's effort is based upon current existence, and nothing proceeds beyond this. Remember, this system flows from the thoughts of men who are the creators, designers, and disseminators of all functions which govern it. Its beauty and attraction are to satisfy the basic human needs in this material world. In fact, socialism borrows (or should I say "steals") much from Christianity, especially from the areas of love, joy, and peace. This is what makes it so appealing to the *materialist*. From the philosophical perspective, this is *a person who supports the theory that nothing exists except matter and its movements and modifications.*[16] Whoever believes in this can have the benefits without any need to form an alliance to some deity or higher being.

We must always beware of those who make promises to take care of us, especially those of the political field. Expect promises for paying our bills, ensuring financial security, providing food, fighting our legal woes, and much, much more. No one can take better care of you than you!

In the Bible, Matthew 24:24 tells us, "For there shall arise false Christs, and false prophets, and shall shew great signs and wonders; insomuch that, if it were possible, they shall deceive the very elect." Included within the deception will be a form of governmental system passed off as Christianity itself, but the primary difference is the population being transformed into a people more dependent upon this system instead of God.

Side-By Side Comparison

... distribution was made unto every man according as he had need. (Acts 4:35b)

... from each one according to his ability to each one according to his needs. (Karl Marx)

Karl Marx's Gotha Slogan basically bears the same interpretative affect, except the Biblical version reflects the love emanating from the people while Marx's view is based upon the mandate of government through force of law.

With all the pretenses of care and concern for human life particularly, the unfettered truth is that socialists only seek to use classes of people to build their organizations and accumulate the power to eventually rule over them. But first, they must win the hearts, minds, and souls through the establishment of a system that convinces the

---

[16] Oxford Languages, 2023, https://languages.oup.com/google-dictionary-en/.

people that they are living in a utopian paradise, or at least this system being touted is the closest thing to it.

At this point, the reason it can be said that socialism is a form of false Christianity is explained by examining two key founding principles that are basically similar, but because of their differing purposes and intentions, place themselves against one another.

In the Bible, the book of Acts gives us insight of not just how the initial church was formed on the Day of Pentecost, but also how it would be maintained in this material world. This short part of Acts 4:35 says, "And distribution was made unto every man according as he had need."

But here is a statement that is quite similar, "From each one according to his ability, to each one according to his needs."

This statement comes from the heart and mind of Karl Marx—an unabashed hater of God and Christianity specifically!

The basis for each system was to establish the way the church and the government must function in everyday life in order to provide service to the people who may need or depend upon them, especially when it comes to individual giving and benevolence. Acts 4 speaks of the members of the first established church, selling their properties and goods to enable the church to take care of fellow members who may have been in some type of need. This unprovoked expression of concern for one another was done by the inspiration of the Holy Spirit. No one commanded or directed them—it was all motivated by love! Christians are expected by Jesus to be generously concerned for the lives and conditions of all men—not just for Christians only. Christian love and charity are never a levy, a mandate, nor an assessment. Even when those who were with wealthy houses, property, and other means, they performed exquisitely simply by volunteering to give, but with the exception of two.

On the other hand, the socialist model was coined by Karl Marx—the father of communism. This is where the two systems that are driven by revenue generation and benevolence redistribution radically part ways. The Acts 4 model is inspired by divine love, while the other is motivated by love for power. The Marxist philosophy is not based upon love but centers upon the use of government force or coercion to extract wealth from one group to give it to another, thus usually generating more love for the governmental system than love for God.

For the Marxists, power was the currency of exchange, but what they exchange for this power is never of themselves. People keep the officials in power, and the officials keep feeding them. Governmental power is derived from the labor and effort of others. As evidenced in practically all of Europe and other western cultures, such as Venezuela that once centered around the Judeo-Christian foundation, the government officials especially have fallen far away from the true Christian faith and have prepared themselves (as we now see today) for generations that will be dependent upon government leaders who will continue to "take care of them" from cradle to grave.

This is another reason why socialism is Christianity's most perfect imposter, but a few things usually occur in order to establish it. First, a group of people are identified as being desperately in need, waiting for the hero to come and rescue them from their oppressive state. Secondly, the hero *creates* a system built upon such promises of deliverance, including being taken care of, is established. The "Chicken in Every Pot" phrase was a form of political sarcasm aimed at Republican presidential candidate by the Democrats during the 1928 election cycle. The phrase painted the illusion that the government would care so much for each home and family that it would guarantee that everyone would be fed and sufficiently cared for.

Then those who are the beneficiaries swear allegiance and total devotion to the system. As it is known, people are creatures of habit. Thus, the socialist trap is sprung with millions of people living dependent upon the system instead of oneself. Is your government so good because of what it provides? Do you consider yourself dependent or independent?

There is a beauty in the system that gives each individual the sense of euphoria.

SOCIALISM REQUIRES VICTIMS

The Black Belt was intended to be the Soviet Union's foothold within the continental United States. The communists intended to cause uprisings and even violent revolutions throughout the southern states where racial unrest was most prevalent. During the closing of the 1930's, Russia and the world's communists envisioned creating the Negro Soviet Republic in the southern part of the United States by harnessing the fear and pain that black people were experiencing from overt racism and the Jim Crow system. The darker portions represent the population density of blacks at that time.

During the closing of the 1930's, Russia and the world's communists envisioned creating the Negro Soviet Republic in the southern part of the United States by harnessing the fear and pain that black people were experiencing from overt racism and the Jim Crow system. The darker portions represent the population density of blacks at that time.

During the first half of the twentieth century, there were some world-changing events that occurred that involved very secretive and clandestine operations. Much of the information was never publicized as it should have been, and our history books are, to this day, anemic in presenting or even containing such information that should have been regarded to be a vital part of our historical record. There were actors working behind the scenes with the objective to cause dissension, unrest, and rebellion even here in the United States but throughout the world.

First of all, wherever you find socialism being touted and practiced, be assured that communism already has a foot in the door. Secondly, wherever you can find these two systems, you will most likely find a group of people who live under some form of insurmountable oppression whether real or imagined. Class warfare had been the most common strategic application for making a population restless to the point of militancy and outright rebellion, especially within traditionally monolithic regions. Along with these issues, America was on the edge for what was known as the Red Scare. In fact, there were actually two periods through which the nation was, as some might describe it, very fearful to the point of being paranoid of communist activity.

The first scare was between 1917 and 1920, and the second was from 1947 to 1957. In either case, the aggression of the socialists and communists in America was actually incalculable! As Vladimir Lenin led the Bolshevik Revolution and overthrew the czarist ruling class system in Russia, he and fellow communists became determined to spread their system across the world with the goal of creating a global communist system of government, and the United States of America was the great pearl to obtain. There would be no God nor Jesus Christ within this new world order. From then onward, religion itself would be a crime punishable by death. An all-powerful central government would rule harshly and decisively because any dissention would be an unwelcomed irritation and quickly removed.

The most effective and efficient method for establishing the socialist system begins with convincing a certain part of the population that they are victims who are in need of deliverance.

As always, socialism always requires a class of victims in order to gain employable and effective influence. But which group or groups could the socialists and communists identify and court in order to gain an inside track? How about classism in South America and racism in the United States?

A key point is that the socioeconomic classes that were prevalent throughout the countries from the colonial period to, still in some cases, today presented an explosive powder keg among the many and various groups of people—both indigenous and settler. From the southernmost tip of the South American continent with Chile, up through the northernmost country of Venezuela; then through Central America and into Mexico, the matter of class has been the essence of social unrest. It always was the rich verses the poor. There was virtually no middle class—only the haves and the have-nots.

However, unlike the monolithic populations where communism had established significantly embedded strongholds, the United States of America was quite a different case. This nation—the melting pot of the world—was unfortunately embroiled in a controversy of itself and of its own making—racism. That which was applied in Europe, Asia, and other parts of the world could not gain much traction within the United States because being a nation that based its economy upon capitalism, people from practically *every* background—whether white, brown, red, yellow, and yes, even black caught the energy of accomplishing the Great American Dream! So the communists sitting in the Kremlin in Moscow had to exploit something besides class warfare—race supremacy.

America's sin was its willingness to neglect the race question without properly asserting the significance of the words of the three great documents—the Holy Bible, the Declaration, and the US Constitution—into the mainstream of American culture and society. This is basically what enabled the socialists to enter into and gain a foothold within much of the black community.

Few people, even blacks in America actually know that they had been targeted by Vladimir Lenin and the global communist movement as far back to around 1938. This effort was not for the purpose of delivering them from the evils of racism and the Jim Crow culture especially in the South. Their primary purpose was to first entice and then support black insurrection and rebellion on the streets of America. In 1938, Russia (pre-Soviet Union) budgeted approximately three hundred thousand. (nearly 6 million dollars in today's calculations) for the purpose of providing financial aid to black, pro-communist groups and leaders. Lenin's organization, called Communist International (COMINTERN) sought to make every nation on earth a communist enclave that would be a part of his one world government system—a new world order. On the most part, the Russian agents identified and located blacks who were already sympathetic toward the communist cause and funded their clandestine activities as well as campus and street protests, militant black organization growth, and violent confrontations.

Manning Johnson, who spent about ten years with the Communist Party USA organization, wrote in his book, *Color, Communism and Common Sense: A True Story*: "For ten years, I labored in the cause of communism. I was a dedicated 'comrade.' All my talents and efforts were zealously used to bring about the triumph of communism in America and throughout the world. To me, the end of capitalism would mark the beginning of an interminable period of plenty, peace, prosperity, and universal comradeship. All racial and class differences and conflicts would end forever after the liquidation of the capitalists, their government, and their supporters. A world union of Soviet States under the hegemony of Russia would free and lead mankind on to Utopia."[17]

Communism's promise of a world free of racism drew Manning Johnson and many other blacks, until he realized that he himself was being victimized by racist policies of the communists themselves. People are never greater than the cause, and unless they can present themselves as some kind of victim class, then they are not of any value. Although he spent a decade working for the communist cause, he—like the prodigal son spoken of in the Bible—finally came to himself, rejected the communist movement in America, and became a staunch enemy to them. After he had published his book in 1958, he unfortunately died in 1959 in California. Some believe mysteriously.

To compliment the communist outreach to black America, some black colleges and universities became ripe for harvesting during those evil times of Jim Crow-ism, unfettered brutality, and apartheid policies. The socialists, closely shadowed by the communist movement, became the sympathetic shoulder for many blacks to lean on and the source for financial backing for practically anything that portrayed the United States as being the nation of hypocrites— and sometimes rightfully so! The pain of racism in the United States was just as debilitating as the class warfare of South America, Europe, and Asia. Though not truly genuine, communism found and took great advantage of the racial unrest throughout America.

There were also many black leaders who devoutly sought ways and methods to make living while black less stressful and more enjoyable. There is a saying observing that "a drowning man will grab anything!" It means that when people are fatalistically desperate, it does not matter what is used to prevent oneself from going under and drowning. It is well known that if a person attempts to rescue

---

[17] Manning Johnson, *Color, Communism and Common Sense: A True Story* (Montana: Lighthouse Trails Publishing Inc., 2021).

another who is desperately flailing and fighting to keep their head above water, there is a certain and immediate notion that the endangered person could easily drown the rescuer while seeking to save themselves. Yes, a desperate person grabs anything—even another person. Black Americans had truly become the nation's victims, and all they needed was a hero!

COMINTERN attempted to be black America's savior during those desperate times of racial uncertainty, and its influential dollars to some of the black leaders and organizations did have some effect. There arose attempts to even create a separate nation or region of black sovereignty and self-determination. History books today do not speak of the Negro Soviet Republic that was supposed to be formed by a belt of counties that stretched from Virginia to East Texas as each one comprised majority populations of blacks.

In a similar fashion, desperate people tend to grab the first or closest thing that would be believed to be able to lift them out of their misery. This is when socialism comes in as the rescuer, whether its poverty or racial hatred. The mistake of those who have the power to lift up or reconcile becomes the reason systems must be defeated and replaced. Vladimir Lenin, Joseph Stalin, Karl Marx, Adolf Hitler, Chairman Mao, Fidel Castro, Hugo Chavez, and all the rest of history's monsters knew this and used humanity's frequent inability to do right against them.

If America's white Christian community would have simply rejected racism, for example, there probably would have not been an extended period of slavery. The Civil War would not have occurred. There would have been no such thing as Jim Crow, and most importantly, the socialist influences within the black communities would have been thoroughly rejected! America would have had to have been perverted by some other method. In essence, having one group of people enjoying life to its fullest, whether in terms of economics or skin color, while others are forced to live beneath the quality of life granted to those privileged, rebellion is certainly inevitable.

As blacks in America struggled with issues such as poverty and racism, it was relatively easy for the communists to approach black colleges and universities, particularly to convince them as well as others to embrace the virtues of socialism. Academia, the universities and think tanks, led black communities into the socialist spider web. One of the first of the great and prestigious institutions of higher learning to do this was President Mordecai W. Johnson and most of the officers at Howard University.[18]

The Marxist assigned to South America and their recruits recognize that the poor were trapped in a two-tier system—the very wealthy and the very poor—meaning two classes of people. Being similar to causing unrest in the United States, the Marxists exploited the disparity between the rich and poor in South and Central Americas as well as surrounding island nations and Mexico.

Fortunately for the United States, even as the activists, university presidents and staff, and other civil rights organizations and groups gave in to the pseudo-compassion exerted toward the suffering black communities, especially in the South, it was the spiritual integrity of the gospel preachers that openly and clearly rejected the courtship of the Marxists. For them, especially in the South, socialism and communism were recognized as being in opposition and direct conflict with Christianity. These ideologies were the essence of evil and against them with scriptures. For this reason, primarily, the Negro Soviet Republic effort collapsed totally. The preacher in the black community had been an overwhelming force.

The matter of class could not be applied in the United States as it did in South America, but there was one form of injustice that became the foundation here of which the Marxists would exploit even to this day—racism. Whether in North or South America, Africa, Europe, Australia, and Asia, the matters of classism and racism became the primary issue that they were easily able to identify and build upon.

Socialism's greatest strategy has been to convince a targeted group of people that they have been "victimized by the system in which they live." One of the most consistent characteristics of social-

---

[18] From the testimony of Professor James A. Cobb, professor of Constitutional Law and vice dean of Howard University. Manning Johnson, *Color, Communism and Common Sense: A True Story* (Montana: Lighthouse Trails Publishing Inc., 2021).

ist activity has been to identify and organize a group of dissatisfied or oppressed people and present themselves as their saviors. For this reason, it can be said that the most blaring evidence of manipulation in modern American history has been the African American population. Once socialism gains the most dominant upper hand, the population in question actually and eventually becomes subservient to the very ones who pretended to rescue them. The rescuing heroes become the lords over the domain. Above all, socialists express interest only in those who further their cause. For example, if a black person in Chicago shoots and kills another black person, the socialist sees no value, thus no interest. On the other hand, if a white policeman shoots and kills a black person, the socialist sees a bonus of issues: gun control, racism, law enforcement authority, political opportunity, and the prolonging of the victimization of the group. This is the basic pattern, including the cycle of victimology.

The socialist strategy for creating and prolonging the victim class includes the manipulation of hatred, fear, envy, jealousy, ignorance, economics, and unrest to maintain control over the group.

Finally, in a manner similar to the days of the slavery of black people in America, socialist elites usually live up and over the people they pretend to exercise dominion over, thus being the primary beneficiaries of the pain and suffering of the victims. They appoint "caretakers" over the meager provisions designated to the victimized class, only giving them enough to survive, but never enough to break free to chart their own courses of life. Every oppressed group has a so-called elitist group or organization representing them. Black America has the NAACP, Black Lives Matter, and many others competing for the finances. The Native Americans have their "representatives." The Hispanics have LULAC and others. But practically every organization that represents "victimized" people have Marxist ties—even the Palestinians have HAMAS, whose billionaire leaders live lavishly in Qatar—safe from the bullets, bombs, and rockets that the people they supposedly represent must face each minute of their lives.

Thus, living under the socialist system renders its "victims" forever dependent and wanting. The great educator and leader, Booker T. Washington (1859–1915), recognized the debilitating influences of victimization as he fought against what was becoming a profitable industry within the black community in its struggle for civil rights. As he witnessed his philosophy of self-sufficiency through learning skills, training and education, he saw his competition being blacks who pushed for instant immersion and insertion into the American culture.

Washington wrote:

> There is another class of coloured people who make a business of keeping the troubles, the wrongs, and the hardships of the Negro race before the public. Having learned that they are able to make a living out of their troubles, they have grown into the settled habit of advertising their wrongs—partly because they want sympathy and partly because it pays. Some of these people do not want the Negro to lose his grievances, because they do not want to lose their jobs.

You can replace the words *colored* and *Negro* in Washington's statement and replace them with any ethnic or racial group; the victimology principle is basically the same!

Finally, this system of perpetual victimization is maintained by feeding the people a steady diet of fear and intimidation, or that which I call *Boo!-ism*. This word represents the sound sometimes used to pretend to be a ghost and shock and frighten an unsuspecting person by shouting boo! In other words, the socialists and their black allies work feverishly to keep their black communities in a state of fear, mistrust and paranoia. For example, boo! there is a klansman behind every tree. Boo! America hates you. Boo! Whites are out to stop you from succeeding. Boo! You cannot make it without us. Racism is used as a haunting apparition that black people in particular must seek help and protection against. So whenever you are being spoken to by a leftist, always look out for the Boo!' Boo!-ism helps to keep black people loyal to the system that has victimized them.

SOCIALISTS LIE

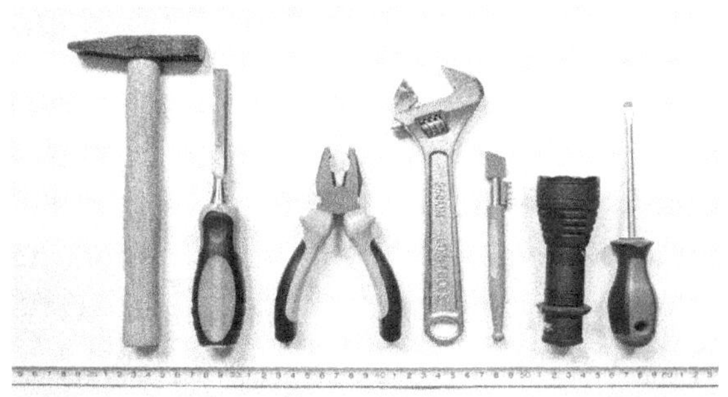

No one who practices deceit will dwell in
my house; no one who speaks falsely will stand in
my presence. (Psalm 101:7 NIV)

One of the most remarkable truths that can be thought about is probably this general statement concerning the purposeful intent of not telling the truth: *lies are always high maintenance.* In other words, a lie—any lie—can never stand alone by itself for any substantial amount of time. It can be hidden, buried, ignored, or even allowed to stand in the presence of men, but it will eventually fall under the crushing weight of its own pretentions. So since there is no God in the socialist mindset, morality becomes subjective, but there must be an attractive form of governing that also pacifies the population into believing that their concerns are being taking care of. This system must be so wonderful that all who come would never want to leave it nor question. Lies begin the fall apart when placed under objective scrutiny.

This system must usually come from out of the current system that is laden with turmoil and excessive stress, like the capitalistic system. It is the most heartless system in which a people could exist! According to the socialist mind, capitalism victimizes the masses, while the wealthy live in total splendor. The notion of hard work is the creed of slaves instead of the self-sufficient and successful entrepreneurs and still-hopeful dreamers. The socialist mantra is that "You cannot make it on your own!"

Every thread of hope and strand of imagination must be captured and redirected into the system for the good of the whole. Whatever it takes to keep you within the confines of the system, they will do it.

The most outstanding character trait of socialists is their unabashed ability to lie and deceive the population in order to further their cause. Please take heed! Unrestrained from the morality of God, the greatest weapon that the socialist has is the unfettered ability to purposely and intentionally lie to the people who trust them without any sense of regret or conscious. Whether a personal one-on-one conversation or speaking to a television audience of tens of millions of people, the willingness to lie can only be limited by the ability to do so. Lies are always high maintenance.

The modern-day teachings of the late Saul Alinsky encourage his disciples to never apologize for anything—never admit it when you are wrong or even having made a mistake. For the socialist ideology, the lie is a useful tool, a formidable weapon, and the ends justifies the means. Now imagine a person whose professional field of work is journalism—an occupation that (according to the Judeo-Christian ethic in America) requires truth, honesty, and the desire to report and avail the facts at all costs. In contrast for example, the journalist in Russia, China, or even a third-world nation would not survive very long with the same set of values. They would be obligated to operate according to the desires or mandates of the state.

Now what do you think about it if a journalist in America was of Marxist or socialist ideology? What if the news anchor of your favorite TV or cable network was not obligated to report to you from the socialist or communist ethic instead of that of the Judeo-Christian? Consider the possibility of your favorite, most trusted news anchor was more concerned about pushing propaganda than just simply telling the truth. The moral code of the socialist is not reflective of the codes established in the traditional American culture. A moral God is offensive if they were pressed about the issue. Therefore, it would not be a stretch of imagination to suggest that today's journalist could be subject and prone to lie to their audience. When people, especially those who are supposed to tell you the truth, willfully and purposefully lie to you, this tells you what they actually think of you. Generally speaking, those who feed the population purposefully deceptive information must always maintain the lie, and the only remedy is confession and then telling the truth. In the Marxist mindset, those they seek to manipulate are not an equal, but only worth what they want you to know. In their minds, that which they lie about is worth more than you. Since there is no God in their universe, morality is fluid and malleable, subject to their own design. The tool chest for maintaining lies is vastly expansive and impersonal, painfully destructive and basically inhumane—capable of afflicting anyone, sparing none. Lies are always high-maintenance.

From Vladimir Lenin's Bolshevik Revolution and Joseph Stalin's Great Purge (Soviet Union), Mao Zedong's Great Leap Forward (China), Fidel Castro's Revolution (China), and Hugo Chavez's Fifth Republic Movement (Venezuela) to today's Democratic Socialists of America organization in the United States, the core mission of these groups has been to turn the citizenship population against government, cause a collapse and reestablish a new system in their own image. Promises of fairness, equality, serenity, and provisions (including health care) are some of the attractions winning great loyalty. Unfortunately, once the socialist system is established, the population gradually realizes that those promises were actually deceptions. But then, it is too late, and freedom is lost possibly forever.

The entire system becomes corrupt and crime ridden as the wealthy and their political-class guardians reap bounties of wealth and benefits while to common masses settle just to live hopelessly in blissful content.

One great dilemma that haunts any individual no matter who they might be, where they are from, or what they might have—lies are always high maintenance. An intentionally false statement cannot stand on its own or, at least, for long. For an ideology or people who have no moral basis or foundation, lying is a fundamental art and, some cases, a résumé enhancement. At this point of the discussion, most individuals are now aware of the truth that deception plays a major role in winning over a population; thus, the employment of instruments, organizations, and individuals ranging from fact-checkers to mainstream media corporations to specifically designed algorithms on the social media platforms engage in search-and-destroy missions for destroying any thought that contradict the message. Lies must be protected at all costs!

Socialism must first deceive the people in order to get into the position of being able to gain the power to control them. Even some of our politicians in America, though dutifully devoted to the teachings of Karl Marx, would never openly admit those positions. Once you've lost your freedom, it may take generations to take it back! We as Americans may foolishly sacrifice our liberty for things and comfort at the ballot box, but as history has already taught, it will most likely take much more to recapture—possibly even blood and bullets.

> He that worketh deceit shall not dwell within my house: he that telleth lies shall not tarry in my sight. (Psalm 101:7)

A stark and obvious example of a government official blatantly lying before our very ears, United States Homeland Security Secretary Alejandro Mayorkas presents an unquestionable example of how flagrant a Marxist or socialist could purposely lie without blinking. His catatonic expressions often make one wonder if there is a conscious mind behind the face of the man as he adamantly insists that there is no crisis at our southern border, in spite of being told of and even shown video clips of the thousands of migrants illegally invading our sovereign lands. He displays no emotions except for a little response to offensive accusations and charges launched at him by those who see the situation as it is.

I submit to you that we are being subjected to a dose of *dialectic reasoning* which comes from the teachings of the world's most diabolical cadre of atheists and Marxists—the intellectuals and executioners who have always dreamed of building the perfect world without God. "A dialectic is when two seemingly conflicting things are true at the same time. For example, 'It's snowing, and it is spring'. You might also see dialectics when in conflict with other people. I like to think of it as having an elephant in the room with two blindfolded people on opposite ends of the elephant."[19]

We must learn enough of this hell-inspired way of thinking in order to bring salvation to our own minds—to courageously resist the assault on truth and rise in glorious victory over the intellectual heathen of this world. From the premise that there is no spiritual (metaphysical) side to existence, socialism's foundation tells us that neither God nor any other deity exists to provide input on how things work in this material world. Therefore, man is the interpreter of all things, and only those who have held fast to what they see as the truth declares them to do it.

Another example of dialectic reasoning is believing that you and an eighteen-wheeler traveling at 70 mph and traveling toward one another cannot be in the same place at the same time! This would be a total catastrophe! *Egalitarianism*, which means having the same outcomes is not the same as *equality* which means having the same opportunity. The Marxist message of having people believe that America can forever allow the unfettered flow of unidentified, unexamined, and unpatriotic illegal immigrants into the country foretells disaster! Dialectic reasoning is designed to create uncertainty in the presence of obvious truth, among other things.

---

[19] Dr. Jillian Glasgow, "A Daily Dose of Dialectics," Broadview Psychology, May 11, 2020, https://broadviewpsychology.com/2020/05/11/a-daily-dose-of-dialectics/.

Anyone with clear, rational thinking and a little common sense can easily see that America's borders (especially the southern border) has been turned into a superhighway for the illegal alien invasion. In addition, the human sex traffickers and the drug cartels have been making billions of dollars. In fact, the drug cartels have begun to depend more on the human smuggling than the drug trade because they can *sell* a human many times over in the forms of prostitution, cheap labor, drug dealing, indentured servitude (slavery), and much more. But Secretary Mayorkas tells us that the borders are under control. Socialists lie with a bold and brazen attitude—even challenging those who see the truth by accusing them of being troubled or mentally disturbed.

Everyone can see that millions upon millions of illegal aliens are flooding across our borders on a daily basis practically unhindered. Secretary Mayorkas has literally stood at the southern US border and declared that the border was under control. We can clearly hear him say that there is no problem at the border, and it *is* under control, but we can also plainly see that the entire situation *is not.* You can use this example of dialectic reasoning to be able to reject politicians and leaders who blatantly lie to gain control over our lives. According to our cultural mores, Secretary Mayorkas is a liar who is lying for the purpose of overwhelming our support systems and is doing a great job promoting the contradiction! But the facts are telling us one thing while Secretary Mayorkas is lying to us with the contradiction. He is attempting to convince us that the contradiction—our southern border—is under control and illegal immigration is the acceptable choice. Joseph Stalin would be proud!

The first statement says that according to our immigration laws, the people who do not enter into this country according to those stipulations are illegal. In contradiction, Secretary Mayorkas says that there is nothing illegal nor wrong with the millions of invaders coming into the land. We know, as he placed his hand on the Bible and swore to "support and defend the Constitution of the United States against all enemies, foreign, and domestic; that I will bear true faith and allegiance to the same; that I take this obligation freely, without any mental reservation or purpose of evasion; and that I will well and faithfully discharge the duties of the office on which I am about to enter. So help me God." This Sec. Alejandro Mayorkas has certainly failed to honor his oath as he boastfully and brazenly lies before the nation as well as the world.

Overall, this system of socialism comes with a strategy based upon removing, purging, and destroying the Judeo-Christian foundation in America as well as any other place in the world where there are a people struggling to gain an atmosphere of liberty or fighting desperately to maintain it. Now this is a very important assignment for you: do not fall for the Marxist tactic of language swapping! First of all, illegal immigration is not about race! It is the imposition of the will of people from other nations upon the sovereignty of the citizens of the United States of America. Through the disregard of our immigration laws and policies, illegal migrants are seeking to force us to accommodate them with any form of customization, training, or preparation.

So how influential has dialectic reasoning been upon American culture today? It is apparent that some of the most controversial issues of our day could be rooted in dialectic reasoning. For instance, can a man have a baby? Should a male compete athletically against a female? Are all whites racist against blacks? Are blacks hopelessly dependent on the government and/or charismatic leaders? Is math racist? Can we define what a woman is? Is Christianity a religion of hate? Are socialism and Christianity compatible? Are mRNA vaccines the only remedies for the COVID-19 pandemic? Does Israel employ apartheid policies against the Palestinians? Each of these questions—just a few among many others—are key arguments that must be understood and mastered in order to effectively challenge the Marxist point of view. Frankly, you will be amazed at how quickly the words of the Marxist/socialist leaders melt away in the light of truth. Such accusations that haphazardly flow throughout the mainstream media, churches, and civic organizations and every level of academia without dissenting voices and those who do speak out are met with loud and shrill attacks, ranging from name-calling to forms of violence up to and including death. Lies must be protected at all costs—they require high maintenance. Empires have been built upon foundations of lies ranging from false deities to flawed policies and principles, resulting in unimaginable damage that brands into the minds of those who learns about each tragic tale. The images of the Nazi extermination camps and the Jonestown, Guyana, suicides both etch themselves into our memories with the same horror.

Here's a final thought concerning the seriousness and depth of depravity we can readily see in the world of academia. Again, I call on John Ellis and his book, *The Breakdown of Higher Education*, as he brought to light a study of the nation's top forty universities in terms of political affiliations across five major fields of study that was conducted by Mitchell Langbert, Anthony Quain, and Daniel Klein. They reported, "We looked up 7,243 professors and found 3,623 to be registered Democratic and 314 Republican, for an overall D:R ratio of 11.5:1. The D:R ratios for the five fields were: Economics 4.5:1, History 33.5:1, Journalism/Communications 20.0:1, Law 8.6:1, and Psychology 17:4:1."[20] Academics has been replaced by activism.

---

[20] John Ellis, *The Breakdown of Higher Education*, 34. This is a 2016 study documenting academia's breakdown into a one-party system.

SOCIALISM AND CHRISTIANITY CANNOT COEXIST

US House Speaker Johnson's self-description was almost immediately met with a tidal wave of unbridled resistance and condemnation, particularly by Jen Psaki, former Biden administration's press secretary and MSNBC's most recent program host to pose the question, "How threatening can this guy actually be?" Her question was the lead-in to a brief video clip by which Speaker Johnson declared:

> I'm a Bible-believing Christian. Someone asked me today in the media. They said…it's curious. "What does Mike Johnson think about any issue under the sun?" I said, "Well, go pick up a Bible off your shelf and read it." That's— that's my worldview.

According to many, US House Speaker Mike Johnson had apparently uttered the most dangerous words a person of any background could say—being a person who not just spoke the rhetoric but truly one who seeks to place principles of God's word into practical application!

Is it threatening because he believes that the Holy Bible is an ample influence on his life and the way he thinks? Credible history could not be told if it were told without any reference to the influences of Holy Writ upon the lives of those who were players and participants in America from its initial discovery and its founding and the decades and centuries, which continually worked to form and more perfect union. But Psaki and those of her leftist ideology vehemently reject a person who seeks to apply God's principles to actual practice. This is a true and real fear of God's word placed into practical application!

> You heard that right! The Bible doesn't just inform his worldview. It is his worldview. In fact during his first speech in his new job, Johnson suggested that his election as Speaker was an act of God! Talk about a bit of humble brag there. So what has God apparently called on Mike Johnson to do? Well, [unintelligible] what you would expect of from a religious fundamentalist. They are more divisive than divine.

Jen Psaki represents the attitude of the vast majority of America's mainstream media, as well as much of journalism's anti-Christian worldview itself. In fact, the majority of the news media's management and staff are greatly overloaded with those of leftist and Marxist ideologies. In other words, socialism and Christianity cannot coexist with one being dominant over the other. Those things that one seeks to build are the very things the other seeks to eliminate. This departure from Christian influence is not unique to America. In fact, this nation has lagged behind much of the European nations.

This is what we who live in the Christian world recognize— spiritual warfare. While some may have determined that we should not mix religion (Christianity) with politics, much of that opinion is based on our departure from our spiritual roots—allowing secularism to drive nation's direction. Politics is the battlefield by which the spiritual warfare of our age is being waged, and in this world, the church is best fit to engage.

Consider the nations and cultures of Europe today, and Great Britain specifically. Socialism abounds! As Christianity spread from Jerusalem and to the uttermost parts of the earth as Jesus had willed, western religion became the standard against even the ancient pagan religions. We received the most common version of the Holy Bible ever translated, the King James Version from the British King's efforts. In spite of some criticisms, one thing that was absolutely positive is that he brought the Bible out of the sole control of the church as it eventually became available even to the most common of men. The subsequent invention of the printing press made it not just increasingly affordable but eventually available to practically every home. Before socialism crept in and overtook Europe, the Christian way of life (though not perfect) helped to literally change the world.

No one could reasonably claim that the Bible has had no influence upon the world, nor has Christianity itself served to influence and affect the arch of human history in a positive way. The vast majority of our greatest philosophers and inventors were individuals who were believers and practitioners of the Christian faith—Ferdinand Magellan, Amerigo Vespucci, Isaac Newton, are only a few of those who were inspired to venture beyond the norm and discover more about God's creation.

Of those persons of historical note, Christopher Columbus is one most intriguing because it was his Christian faith that propelled him to do so much of what he did in the New World to spread the Gospel of Jesus Christ. Few people know of his writing called *Book of Prophecies*. An excerpt from the book says, "For more than forty years, I have sailed everywhere that people go. I prayed to the most merciful Lord about my heart's great desire, and he gave me the spirit and the intelligence for the task: seafaring, astronomy, geometry, arithmetic, skill in drafting spherical maps and placing correctly the cities, rivers, mountains, and ports. I also studied cosmology, history, chronology, and philosophy. It was the Lord who put into my mind (I could feel his hand upon me) the fact that it would be possible to sail from here to the Indies."

Other writings tell us that Columbus was also determined to spread the gospel. For example, he described the natives of the Bahamas as being "friendly and well-dispositioned," having "handsome bodies and very fine faces," their "docility." He then concluded,

"I think they can easily be made Christians, for they seem to have no religion."[21]

Even more, Columbus in credited to have ended cannibalism in the West Indies! The Arawak people were hunted and slaughtered by the Carib tribe to the point of near extinction. It was the effort of the Europeans and their settling of this part of the world that brought civility, despite the truth that some of the explorers were more conquistadores than evangelicals. Legitimate arguments can easily flow back and forth, but the ultimate and eventual outcome brought forth a great nation that has delivered much good into a dark and barbaric world. If this is a preposterous gesture, then explain why although there are about 195 countries in the world, about 170 of them are represented as illegal immigrants at America's southern border!

Let us admit that of the great explorers and inventors, none of these men were perfect—they were as human then as we are today—laden with as many burdens and sinful thoughts as any of us would be today. From Adam to Moses, the Apostle Paul to Rev. Dr. Martin Luther King, we will find that their contributions toward the furtherance and betterment of the human condition far outweighs their own faults. Our problem is a term called *presentism*, which basically means looking back into ancient history especially and seeking to apply our morals and judgments to those persons of those times. Today, the revisionists seek to describe these great men and women as being more evil than good, more devilish than Christian. Why do they do this? It is because their morality is different from ours—the principles given to us by God. The principles driving the revisionist agenda uses lying to sever us from the truth in order to make Marxism the basis for our living. I hold this position with great commitment and a resolve of steel because, as a person of color, I was totally blown away when I gained access to the wealth of knowledge regarding the unedited history of the very founding of this nation—including the participation of black people in the American Revolution. My own personal quest for truth gave me the drive and energy to seek out and

---

[21] Log of Christopher Columbus, transcribed by Robert Fuson (Maine: International Marine Publishing Corporation, 1987), p. 73–79.

find much more! Remember, it is the truth that makes us free, while the goal of untruth is to place and keep us in bondage.

But what happened to those strong and indominable Christian influences once so prevalent in Great Britain, as well as the European culture as a whole? At one time, those influences brought Europe particularly out of the shadows of its pagan cultures. Spiritual darkness became impenetrable light. The Christian Bible's influence eventually transformed much of the continent and the world itself into a sense of God-consciousness that stressed having a unique, personal relationship with him by which no other person—not even a king or queen—had right to interfere with. Just as the Ten Commandments and the law of Moses brought forth a nation of people dedicated to God, the Israelites, Christianity's impact on the world has been immeasurably good for the human experience. The concept of all men being created by this one, all-powerful being started to take root in western Europe, and from that there eventually emerged a group of trans-Atlantic voyagers seeking to establish themselves as a free-willed colony of servants in the new world.

In fact, it was the founding of the United States of America which eventually came forth to lead the world from a moral and righteous point of view. From within the experiences of its own *growing pains* of the American Revolution, the Civil War, the Civil Rights Movement, and the emergence of a strong and viable middle class, it was the Judeo-Christian ethic that caused this nation to acquire its own uniqueness while other nations became bridled with the dependency more upon men and governments.

In the populations of the European nations today, socialism abounds while religion in general (except for Islamism) is on life support. According to the Pew Research Center, the trending for Christianity strongly suggests that it is in fast decline. Among the Christians in the United Kingdom, France and Germany for example, only 10 to 12 percent of them say that their religion is the most important thing in their lives as compared to 68 percent of the Americans (which used to be over 80 percent). In addition, several nations of Latin America and sub-Saharan Africa reflect a stronger adherence and devotion to their faith. For example, citizens of Bolivia, Peru, Ecuador, and Colombia generally state that their Christian faith is the most important part of their lives, ranging from 73 to 80 percent.[22]

It is apparent that the strength (or weakness) of Christianity itself has been directly proportional to the amount of government involvement and intervention in the daily lives of the populace. In other words, the more *benefits* offered, the greater the eventual and ultimate dependency upon the provider. A subsequent observation in this area of discussion is this: dependency redirects the individual's reliance upon one's own self away from them toward another source. The more successful the government is in *creating* a utopian way of life, the less likely those benefitting from it will seek neither God nor any spiritual or metaphysical source for guidance or inspiration. People become convinced that the government is the only source of all things and none other.

Remember, socialism is the courtship period between the citizens and the ruling authority or government. The lesser the individual had to worry about their daily needs, the more compliant and submissive they became with the providing government agency. The result is the destruction of the individual's drive for self-sufficiency. Innovation and ingenuity are destroyed. Imagination becomes bound and controlled, subject to punishment if it ventures outside of the boundaries. For these and other reasons, we should carefully study the lives of those who live in or have departed from socialist and communist nations to come to America as well as considering how the Great Society and it's welfare programs have all but obliterated the Black family structure, including having created a degree of enmity between the Black male and female.

In other words, the greater one depends upon the government system, the less reliant is one's ability to provide for oneself. For each human being, there is a spark within that becomes all but extinguished. This spark emits the light of innovation, ingenuity, creativity, and many other virtues that propel humanity itself as a whole. It

---

[22] "The Age Gap in Religion around the World," Pew Research Center Surveys, 2008–2017.

is said that "Where there is no vision, the people perish." The inspiration of the *master* will be reflective of the fruit that is sought after.

For example, most people are aware of, or have at least heard about, the list of rules given to the Hebrew people through Moses known as the Ten Commandments. In Matthew 22:36–40, Jesus was asked the question of which commandment was the greatest one:

> Master, which is the great commandment in the law? Jesus said unto him, "Thou shalt love the Lord thy God with all thy heart, and with all thy soul, and with all thy mind. This is the first and great commandment." And the second is like unto it, "Thou shalt love thy neighbor as thyself." On these two commandments hang all the law and the prophets.

So God's most urgent requirement or expectation has been, is, and shall always be for humanity to *love.* Love him, love others, and love yourself! This is the essence of who we are as Americans— to care for the needy, to feed the hungry, help the helpless, and so forth. From one end of the earth to the other, this is who we are! We have been the only nation that has defeated an enemy in war, stayed there to help them rebuild, and then left without seeking to exercise dominion and control.

On the other hand, a brief examination of nations and cultures built upon socialism tells us that the human being must love the government above all else or the figurehead who represents that power. Germany's god, Adolf Hitler, started with socialistic principles and rewarded its dependents most for contributing toward the Nazi war machine, including the numerous and various ways to kill people who were deemed inferior. Joseph Stalin's Russia, which became the Soviet Union first, won the hearts of the common people with his courtship, but then crushed tens of millions once he acquired full power. While the God of the Holy Bible, the God of the Torah, the God of Abraham, Isaac and Jacob has always sought to manifest the best of humanity through his governance, fallible men have sought to do the same without him. For this humanity, God must decrease so that the human leader or figurehead could increase!

So let us take a closer look into this. During the eighteenth century, the luminaries of the Enlightenment movement, on the most part, had issued a public declaration of independence from God and his priests, as well as emperors and kings. It was also fortunate that not all these individuals sought to dismiss God or religion in general from the discussion but journeyed in the opposite direction as they sought to understand theology themselves instead of being forced by edict to accept and live according to the authority. They have left indelible marks within the annals of history—some very beneficial but some extremely fatalistic.

This newfound freedom of the human spirit then became, among other things, the battle plan for the war of attrition against the higher powers of their day (for example, czars, kings, and popes) that began with the American and French Revolutions. The major difference was that some sought religious consolation while others sought total rejection of it even as a reality. "The outcome of this conflict was settled from the start, and already in the early nineteenth century, the center of gravity in European life had shifted from problems of faith to those of class, industrialization, urbanization, nationalism, and colonialism. The 'long' nineteenth century, from the French Revolution to World War I, culminated in a crisis involving all these new factors, and the result was total war in the twentieth. After this catastrophe, Europe was divided geographically and ideologically, but still unified in believing that the challenge of religion was over. Since World War II, Europeans have stared in blank amazement across the Atlantic at a new global power whose citizens and even leaders seem to believe myths about the old-bearded man in the sky. They call this American 'exceptionalism,' on the assumption that living without God is the ultimate destiny of the human race."[23]

In the Bible, we can see how the nation of Israel became so intently enamored with the desire to be like the nations surrounding

---

[23] Mark Lilla, "Europe and the Legend of Secularization," *New York Times*, March 31, 2006.

them, particularly in the area of the authoritative position of king. The Egyptians, the Hittites, Philistines, and Assyrians were governed by kings—men who reigned and ruled the nations for thousands of years. This *royalty* tended to have been hereditary, meaning that the throne of power was usually held by a particular family unless an overthrow ended the reign of one family, only to be extended by the usurper's lineage. For these cultures, the rulership became based upon divine right, mandating that it was the will of deity to appoint individuals to the throne to rule over them.

So as the surrounding nations, Israel's desire was to become like them—to have a king to lead them. Israel rejected God for a king. Their only salvation rested in whether that king followed God or sought to rule according to his own will and the results were devastating! However, other examples reflective of human choices tell similar stories. On July 4, 1776, America's Founding Fathers rejected a king for God, suggesting quite different outcomes. The French Revolution was credited to have been officially started on May 5, 1789. The French rejected both God and king for human wisdom—a form of secular humanism. On March 8, 1917, the country of Russia rejected the czar (king) for a system similar too but much harsher than the French. This is known as the Bolshevik Revolution. Man's self-confidence in governing himself has been devastating.

The Enlightenment era brought both positive and negative impact and into the world. Some may view this period as the time when man came into the awareness of his full and unlimited potential—a being having gained greater and total comprehension of who he is as well as being capable of becoming even more. The majority of the Enlightenment alumni were absolutely and completely done with religion and followed the path of materialistic quests instead of laying fault on God instead of those men who were in error.

It was thought during the Enlightenment that human reasoning could discover truths about the world, religion, and politics and could be used to improve the lives of humankind. Skepticism about received wisdom was another important idea; everything was to be subjected to testing and rational analysis. Religious tolerance and the idea that individuals should be free from coercion in their personal lives and consciences were also Enlightenment ideas.[24] This included making personal decisions and judgments aside from divine guidance and wisdom—especially the thousands of years of the Bible's Old and New Testament history.

The luminaries of this age were obviously capable of exerting extraordinary influence over much of the known civilized world. With France being the epicenter of unbridled and unrestrictive thought being performed—free of any clerical or monarchial authority, they drove ideas, philosophies, scientific theories and discoveries of the period by widely circulating their ideas and displaying their *genius*. There were venues which fertilized and incubated the meetings of the minds included, such venues as scientific academies, Masonic lodges, literary salons, coffeehouses, and published their thoughts in printed books, journals, and pamphlets became the common theater for the academic and intellectual elites. From this time came a variety of movements including liberalism, neoclassicism, and yes, socialism. Nations and cultures would absorb the genius of the illuminated ones into their institutions of academia as well as those of science and medicine.

Because the ultimate goal of the purveyors of this socialistic ideology has always been to control *all* governments and global systems, there cannot be any belief system that competes with it, and since this philosophy actually poses as or imitates the Judeo-Christian ethos, there is no surprise that the Christian faith is its primary target for elimination. Besides seeing men as beings having divine or godlike qualities (i.e., Adolf Hitler, Vladimir Lenin, Joseph Stalin, Mao Zedong, Frederick Engels, Fidel Castro, Hugo Chavez, etc.), each system required human interaction and participation, but each one differed in this most important way: Christianity is built upon each individual's free-will choice, from believing in a greater supreme being who is intelligent and all-powerful. Accepting Jesus Christ as Savior and Lord to one's daily walk as a believer in his teachings. On

---

[24] What Were the Most Important Ideas of the Enlightenment?" Britannica, https://www.britannica.com/question/What-were-the-most-important-ideas-of-the-Enlightenment.

the other hand, socialism is based upon each individual being forced to participate by living as according to the "leadership" and rules of the one(s) who is above and over all.

As history has consistently shown, "socialism, no matter how many times it has been tried, always fails." The promises of government provisions have always been the bait that had ensnared nations and its people. The lure of creating a utopian society without God, or a heaven on earth, has led to the slaughter of over 100 million innocent souls. Our trajectory as a nation is not intended to follow the fatal paths of the other great empires of the past which have risen to greatness and either abruptly collapsed or corroded slowly from the internal rust of immorality and self-aggrandizement. God's Word is designed to make us better—a more perfect union—destined to present ourselves as a shining city on a hill instead of a deep, dark pit that entraps and enslaves wandering souls.

Therefore, let us acknowledge that the United States of America has been built upon the foundational principles of the Holy Bible of the Judeo-Christian faith. Our faith teaches us that there is only one triune God—God the Father, God the Son, and God the Holy Spirit. There is one Savior Jesus the Christ—the Anointed One of God who was crucified (sacrificed) for the sinful state of all men, and finally, the Holy Spirit whose indwelling presence within the hearts of those who believe in Jesus's perfect work on the cross. Opposite the world of materialism, we look toward eternal life under the authority of the one eternal Kingdom of God that exists above all else, and the final demise and punishment of our primary adversary named Satan, the devil after his own fleshly manifestation, the Antichrist, makes a final attempt to rule the world by deceiving the world and impersonating Jesus.

Why does he impersonate Jesus? It is because as Christianity teaches, Jesus is the Son of God, meaning that he is the physical manifestation of the one true living God, creator of all things. Like the image in a mirror, the Antichrist will be the son of Satan, the devil made flesh. So closely will the Antichrist's appearance resemble Jesus, untold numbers of people will follow him, believing that he is the Messiah! His power will not come from heaven but will be based upon the rule of government.

This means that according to biblical doctrine, a form of socialism *will be* the domain of the Antichrist figure yet to come, but his spirit is influencing many people and nations as the spiritual warfare is being waged against the Church even today.

So when we consider Europe, in comparison to as it was before Enlightenment and as it is today, the effects are tremendously apparent. Socialism has certainly replaced Christianity to a significant degree. In the battle for the hearts of men, they cannot coexist. Neither can there be a truce nor a standoff. Everything is absolute, either and or. We have two *all-powerful* entities desiring to be worshipped in this world. One is worthy, but one is not.

To religious officials, something needs to be done and now, before even more of the once-sacred structures are repurposed for clothes shops, climbing walls, or nightclubs, is a phenomenon seen over much of Europe's Christian heartland, from Germany to Italy and many nations in between. It really stands out in Flanders, in northern Belgium, which has some of the greatest cathedrals on the continent and the finest art to fill them. If only it had enough faithful. A 2018 study from the Pew research group showed that in Belgium, of the 83 percent of respondents who say they were raised Christian, only 55 percent still consider themselves so. Only 10 percent of Belgians still attended church regularly.[25]

The issue has not only affected Belgium, but every European nation operates in a similar manner—having experienced a certain departure from religious belief and tradition. Practically every country of the European continent shares the same story of straightforward secularism where churches and religious facilities are now more likely to be converted into practically everything except for them remaining places for worship.

With the advent of the European Union (EU) in 1993, any of the estimated four hundred forty-eight million people today are

---

[25] Raf Casert, "In Europe's Empty Churches, Prayer and Confessions Make Way for Drinking and Dancing," *Los Angeles Times*, June 22, 2023.

citizens, meaning that they have the right to freely move within any of the twenty-seven countries without concern about discrimination for which of the EU countries they came from. Like the state-to-state relationships within the United States, each citizen is guaranteed the same or, in some cases, greater consumer protections and health care benefits in fellow member nations of the EU.

For the socialist movement to be effectively established in the United States, the process of eliminating Christianity from the public square must be priority number one. If this does happen, then the entire foundation of the nation would be destroyed and refashioned in the image of men. This paradigm shift would include an entire rewriting of laws and social codes. Good would most likely become evil and much of what is right would become wrong.

> For what is a man profited, if he shall gain the whole world, and lose his own soul? Or what shall a man give in exchange for his soul? For the Son of man shall come in the glory of his Father with his angels; and then he shall reward every man according to his works. (Matthew 16:26–27)

SOCIALISM IMPRISONS AND DESTROYS THE HUMAN SPIRIT

George Orwell's Animal Farm was a very descriptive novel detailing socialism's step-by-step process for overthrowing authority and replacing it with leaders who became the heartlessly cruel and greedy ruling elite.

The 1954 novel *Animal Farm* by George Orwell tells the story of a group of farm animals who rebelled against their seldom sober owner, farmer Jones. They went as far as attacking him and literally drove him off of his farm and established a system of living for all the farm animals that were there. The chickens, horses, donkeys, ducks, geese, and all the other animals formed an alliance against Jones and the group of men seeking to help him recapture his farm.

After repelling a counterattack, the animals then set up a system of government that was initially based upon the universal creed, "All animals are equal." No creature was to live nor be better, greater, nor more important than the other. Farmer Jones's land was now to be the perfect place—the utopian society. This new place was to be much better than any other farm because the animals owned it now, not Jones.

Everyone who lived on the farm was excited about the concept of all animals being equal. Sounds familiar? The place had become the envy of the entire region—so perfect that the pigs had a fence built around the entire property, convincing the animals that it was necessary in order to keep animals from other farms from trying to get into their paradise.

It was the pigs that had led the rebellion, and they set the rules. They claimed the farmhouse as their own and assigned increasingly laborious tasks: more production, less food consumption. Generally, the farm animals became poorer, but the pigs became fatter and lazier. Food was rationed to the other farm animals while the wasteful pigs lived lavishly. Any animal who asked questions or became suspicious mysteriously disappeared. The pigs had also trained vicious guard dogs to protect them against any other animal who challenged them. The utopia had become a prison because even the fence that was supposed to keep others out was actually meant to keep them in. Boxer, the loyal horse in the novel, was a tragic hero. His undying loyalty in "working harder" at the behest of the ruling class of pigs caused him to literally work himself to death as he finally collapsed from exhaustion and was sold to the glue factory. It was a demoralizing moment as the animals saw him being carried away to be slaughtered for glue. Boxer and many others had outlived their worth for the farm system—like those who no longer produce for the government.

Eventually, the farm animals rebelled and overthrew the reign of the pigs, but of all the laws the pigs had established, the final and supreme law was "All animals are equal, but some are more equal than others." The pigs never had anything of themselves to give. The ducks, geese, and chickens were able to give eggs. The horses and donkey were able to pull wagons and lift and carry loads, the sheep, goats and cattle gave wool and milk, and so forth. But a pig could not give a ham or a slice of bacon with making the ultimate sacrifice!

They callously and heartlessly used and abused the productivity and hope of the others for their own good pleasure. They had set themselves up to be *more equal* than the other farm animals and had been secretly living in total luxury and splendor.

Within a "closed society," such as in *Animal Farm*, we will find a small group of leaders who enslave the vast majority of its citizenry. It happens every time! Although the Black Lives Matter movement and subsequent organization made hundreds of millions of dollars, allowing its founders and leaders to live lavishly and purchase homes in communities they supposedly spoke out against, it is said that not one penny went toward payment of funeral expenses for the individuals and families they were supposedly in support of. Even as Israel and Gaza are being ripped apart by war and the Palestinian people suffer with extreme poverty and homelessness, their chosen leaders of HAMAS live lavishly as billionaires in Qatar. Yes, Islamic-Marxism is a form of socialism.

It is somewhat ironic to personify farm animals to illustrate the potential plight of people who believe that they can establish a perfect world by self-sufficiency and dedication to the cause, but George Orwell's novel was written in the light of the human infatuation with itself. It's even acceptable to be miserable as long as everyone else is. It is a part of human nature. Neither God nor monarch was needed to produce the better side of men. All it took was *mutual agreement!* The socialist or communist movement had finally begun to flex its muscles and roar as a lion in the most civilized places in this world.

Human nature can be as mysterious as a *black hole*—that region in deep space where the gravitation pull is so strong that not even light can escape it. Science (as it should be) is fascinated about its secrets as we often wonder what can come in or out of one. The human mind can be a mystery, as vast as the universe itself. Yet, on the other hand, human nature also can be more predictable than the sun rising in the morning. What a vast contrast human beings can display! People can become addicted to practically anything, including drugs, money, gambling, foods, other people—practically anything, even laziness! Usually, the addicted does not come into this condition alone. For example, the first crack rock placed into the person's hand is free. Then comes the prison addiction. The lure of living an easy life has been humanity's quest since the Garden of Eden. Man has always sought to fight against whatever constrains him—even God. However, in light of this innate urging, consider the epic journey of a group of people we know as the Pilgrims.

The most daunting endeavor in world history has to be the saga of the journey of the group of commoners known as the Pilgrims, who were led from Europe (Holland) across the Atlantic Ocean in search of a place where they the Puritans could worship God as they saw fit. Having been squeezed by the strict mandates of Catholicism on one side and King James's aggressive campaign of arresting and imprisoning those called Separatists on the other. This group of faithful and determined voyagers became known as Pilgrims. They desperately sought the freedom to worship and serve God free of the rigorous servitude of the Church of England, which was yet steeped in the vestiges of Catholic ritualism and influence.

After seeking refuge in the Netherlands, they found the Dutch accommodating and tolerant of their religious practices but soon became wary of the culture's influence upon their youth. They finally made plans to venture to the New World, and in September of 1620, they started out from Plymouth, England, toward Northern Virginia, the place where they believed that they would find true liberty for themselves and future generations.

The 66-day voyage from England to North America was an extremely rugged and treacherous ordeal for the 102 passengers aboard the Mayflower, with rough seas featuring towering waves and bone-piercing winds. Instead of reaching colony at Virginia, the Mayflower had been blown off course, arriving at Plymouth, Massachusetts, instead. The passengers were not allowed to simply disembark. Some of the men had to leave the ship in groups to explore what was in the area.

When the decision to leave the Mayflower and settle there at Plymouth, there had to be a written agreement—a social contract had to be created, discussed, agreed on and signed by the men who qualified this legal document. Each man had to sign the contract and before leaving the ship, the voyagers came to an agreement as to how they were to govern themselves, and William Bradford created a document of settler agreement known as the Mayflower Compact, which was signed on November 21, 1620.

William Bradford and the leaders designed and presented a system of living for the settlers that was modeled after the New Testament church in the Bible. Everyone was to work for the *good of the whole*. It was a form of socialism. Every person was supposed to help contribute to the *common good* of all. For example, the men hunted and placed their meats into a common place for storage; they also farmed and grew crops with the same result. Likewise, the women performed chores, cooked, and harvested with the same purpose. As Bradford and the leaders of the settlers sought to imitate what had occurred on the Day of Pentecost in Act chapter 4:

> And the multitude of them that believed were of one heart and of one soul: neither said any of them that ought of the things which he possessed was his own; but they had all things common.

> And with great power gave the apostles witness of the resurrection of the Lord Jesus: and great grace was upon them all. Neither was there any among them that lacked: for as many as were possessors of lands or houses sold them, and brought the prices of the things that were sold, and laid them down at the apostles' feet: and distribution was made unto every man according as he had need.

Although this may have been a valiant and faithful effort, this plan to operate the new Pilgrim settlement at Plymouth, Massachusetts, illustrated how men can so easily seek to establish a system of mutually caring for one another but fail to sustain it. It can never be enforced because it is designed to operate through the individual's own free will, inspired by the Holy Spirit. Bradford's effort was actually turned out to be an early version of socialism. Several things began to develop within the system that caused it to fail. Issues such as resentment and responsibility began to set in. For example, the young men did not believe that it was fair to take care of the chores for the widows at the expense of their own homes and families. When it came to planting and harvesting, some shirked their duties but sought to receive just as much harvest as those who labored more.

Men were unwilling to work to feed someone else's children. Women were unwilling to cook for other women's husbands. Fields lay largely untilled and unplanted. Famine came as soon as they ate through their provisions. After famine came plague. Half the colony died. Unlike most socialists, they learned from their mistakes, giving each person a parcel of land to tend to for themselves. The colonists threw off the statist intellectual fashions of their day.[26]

In his journal, Bradford observed, "By the spring, our food stores were used up, and people grew weak and thin. Some swelled with hunger. So they began to think how they might not still thus languish in misery."[27]

So Bradford's initial effort to cause the people to selflessly do for others, particularly for those who were not of one's own immediate family kinship, led to total system failure. Instead of inspiring the good, it brought out the bad. There had to be something greater than themselves—a higher calling of purpose even greater than the system Governor Bradford had instituted. The *love* they had for each other had waxed cold!

To solve this matter, Governor William Bradford assigned parcels of land for each family to farm for themselves, giving each of them the autonomy to dispose of their produce as they saw fit. Even

---

[26] Based on the memoirs of Plymouth governor, William Bradford, the article "Thanksgiving Lessons about the Failures of Socialism and the Success of Private Property and Capitalism" by Mark J. Perry. Jerry Bower, "Lessons from a Capitalist Thanksgiving," *Forbes*, November 27, 2008, https://www.forbes.com/2008/11/27/thanksgiving-economy-history-oped-cx_jb_1127bowyer.html.

[27] Jerry Bower, "Lessons from a Capitalist Thanksgiving."

the craftsmen were able to make and sell or trade their products with other settlers.

To prevent this tragedy from reoccurring, Governor Bradford decided to "set corn every man for his own particular. Assigned every family a parcel of land." This change from a communal system to private ownership totally transformed the entire outlook of the journey from Europe to America! There was a natural incentive for the families to *work hard* in order to receive the blessings of their labor. Governor Bradford concluded that this change "made all hands very industrious, so as much more corn was planted than otherwise would have been."[28] The production became so fruitful that the colonists were able to trade with the natives.

Did Bradford become tyrannical and established a ruling elite like the pigs in George Orwell's *Animal Farm*? Did he seek to demean or live above the settlers as they labored to preserve the colony? This was obvious. Although they had tried to install a system of government that was an experiment in socialism, Bradford recognized that the wisdom of God was greater. What he did—giving each family a parcel of land—actually brought out the good qualities that caused them to be inspired and productive. They worked "for themselves" and were able to do so much more for others. Socialism buries the human spirit and extracts the best for its greater good instead of waiting for that which individuals can offer freely. Bradford's incentive became the driving force for initiative, and a new nation pregnant with new ideas and concepts was born!

In America, as well as any other industrialized culture, we see thousands of homeless people strewn along the city streets and roadways. The urban areas would also have recreational parks that have become settlements for those who call no place home as every niche and cranny is filled with someone or somebodies as space allows. Misery, filth, and disease accompanies each individual as mental health issues are the only barriers that prevent them from truly realizing how miserable they actually are.

---

[28] Jerry Bower, "Lessons from a Capitalist Thanksgiving."

It is often reasoned that the overwhelming majority of these unfortunate individuals are actually very intelligent fellows but for some reason have fallen between the proverbial cracks. Some are highly educated, and many have extremely wealthy backgrounds or come from affluent families. Some, at one time, were university professors and others were CEOs. One might come across a homeless person with a computer-like brain but is now mentally locked in repetitive phrases and actions. Used needles that were given to users by organizations or ministries that *cared* matt the pathways. Spending most of their days under the influence of one thing or another, most of the unfortunate individuals wander around their area and territory aimlessly lost within themselves and imprisoned in this state of lostness, deprived of remembering who they actually are. One might ask, "How did they get themselves into this situation—this slough of hopelessness?"

Los Angeles, San Francisco, Denver, Austin, Houston, New York, and practically every major city is shackled with the plight of helpless and homeless people. The matter has become so serious that it strains the budgets of practically every city as well as charitable organizations. The number of homeless people seems to be exploding geometrically and even spreads out from the urban areas into rural communities. Then this is more challenging because of the unending waves of illegal immigrants flowing primarily across our southern border.

The aforementioned cities as well as others can be identified with one thing in common: practically all are controlled or influenced by liberal or socialist leaders who are more interested in supplying the hypodermic syringes than facilitating real cures and restoration!

Yes, there are leaders who have forsaken or have actually rejected this nation's history and traditions which, on the most part, have catapulted the United States far ahead of other nations that have existed for over three hundred years—with Europe specifically in mind. It is obvious that individual freedom and the benefits of personal liberty has been a significant factor. In a comparatively short time span, the United States of America has been the most prolific nation of people who have excelled in the arts, science and technology, agriculture, sports, and so much more. An individual can come from an economically destitute third-world country and become a millionaire or at least join the ranks of the middle class. It is America and its capitalist system that has its own built-in incentive of motivations that inspire individuals to follow their dreams and visions, think outside of the box, and allow them to utilize their own God-given gifts and talents to rise to wealth, prosperity, and stardom!

On the other hand, socialism does not provide such an opportunity for the average person. In the socialist system, there are those who may not be homeless because their needs are being taken care of by the system. Each month, or whatever regular interval, there is a unique dynamic that is energized by tens of millions of financial transactions around the world or through some form of federal mail delivery system—from the government to the dependent person.

In either case, whether one is homeless or a beneficiary of the welfare system, there is a loss of potential for the individual to strive and excel above any adversity. Personal incentive slowly dies. The motivation for a person to work for reward is not a bad thing, but the welfare system does very little to promote or encourage them to do so. In fact, it is a gratifying experience when the individual is able to place value upon their own personal labor in comparison to what is earned, but there is a penalty for doing so. The socialist welfare system is a disincentive for the individuals, and even the monthly stipend causes the individual to actually live *down* to that level of life it affords. There are millions of young men and women who forget about their dreams and plans for success and survive according to the low-income level the stipend provides.

This is a direct result of President Lyndon Johnson's War on Poverty campaign in the Observation No. 1 section. For over sixty years, many young females—especially in the minority communities—did not dream of graduating from high school and then attending institutions of higher learning to obtain college degrees and starting life-sustaining careers as professionals. As teenagers, they hope and plan to have at least one baby to qualify for federal and state benefits. Tragically, all of this has been carefully crafted without any incentive to keep the male involved.

In this system, individualism is a serious crime, with the perpetrator being subjected to harsh punishment that can range from social ostracism to in the most repressive nations, including imprisonment or death itself! Each person is conditioned and brainwashed to be humble and submissive to the state—willing to report *anyone* to the authorities who dare to be different. In addition, each person is directed to live according to his or her value to the state itself and never to seek personal wealth, prosperity, or success. Capitalism is worse than individualism because there cannot be one without the other.

The will to pursue one's own dream or simply attempt to keep a little more for oneself is seen as being selfish and immoral, thus relegating the entire population to serve the state and its elite class that thrives is the best of all things. The majority of these individuals eventually lose the drive for life, liberty, and happiness and settle to simply live and be like everyone else. Contrary to God's word, each individual has been given certain gifts which enable him or her to successfully function in this world (Romans 12:6–8), first in the secular world, and when the person becomes a Christian believer, those basic gifts become fully developed for the operation of the church and the glory of God. This cannot happen when or if the individual becomes dependent upon the government system which controls how they "live, move, and have their being." Socialism is a courtship between the government and the people, who depend upon it to the point that they are enslaved. Remember that *nothing is free*.

In reflection of those verses in Acts 4, we must recognize that the events that occurred during that time was something uniquely reserved to the church. As it recorded that the people sold all their properties and brought to proceeds to the Apostles, those funds were to be used exclusively for first, the daily operation of the church itself; secondly, the church's work of giving to those who had need did not simply cause the recipients to become helpless waifs who consistently waited for daily morsels of benefits. The bread crumb existence is *not* the goal of the Body of Christ!

These provisions of benevolence also provided opportunities to repair and restore broken lives. There were still wealthy individuals and families to come and be part of Jesus's work. Some were very successful businessmen and women. Some were Romans, some were Jewish—they were of every known race and ethnicity from every part of the known world. There was no vow of poverty, just to learn how it was to love one another.

From the very conception that men could live in a society where they would perform in the same manner as bees or ants with each one *knowing his or her place* would always and eventually be destined for failure—with devastating results. We are not insects, nor are we to be considered so predictable that we can be confined to another's determination of who we are and what we are to do! The most devastating part of any socialist system is that it is actually ruled by a class of elitists who basically live outside of the rules they make.

The socialist system cannot afford to have free-thinking individuals outside of the class of elites. In contrast, Christianity is powered by freethinkers who allow Jesus to guide them through the indwelling presence of the Holy Spirit. For the socialist, the notion of all men being created equal is a myth. Darwin's evolutionary theory (in the socialist mind) has established this as their absolute truth, and anyone who disputes this must be silenced and penalized. However, the nature of the human clamors for freedom and liberty, having no man to determine his destiny. The person who dwells in complacency within the socialist bubble can live their entire life there or until there comes a need for more. That's when the trouble begins!

> Stand fast therefore in the liberty wherewith
> Christ hath made us free and be not entangled
> again with the yoke of bondage. (Galatians 5:1)

THE FINAL SOLUTION FOR SOCIALISM IS DEATH

COMMUNIST/SOCIALIST DICTATORS WHOSE FINAL SOLUTIONS ENDED IN MASSIVE DEATHS

During the first half of the twentieth century, the entire planet became engulfed with wars that were never before seen or experienced because of man's ability to mechanize the ability to kill. The technological advancements gave men the ability to kill people on an industrialized scale. The first great war, appropriately named World War I, was officially started with the assassination of a Bosnian Serb named Gavrilo Princip, who assassinated Archduke Franz Ferdinand and his wife Sophie, Duchess von Hohenberg. This was the catalytic moment that started a series of moves that ended up launching the war.

Twenty-one years later, the second war, allegedly being the "war to end all wars," was built upon the technological advancements in warfare that made it much more efficient to kill. The estimated human death toll was 15 million military personnel and over 38 million civilians. WWII was centered around the ideology and fervent believe that Germany was the center for the continued and accelerated evolutionary advancement of the human race. The most critical part of this belief became the justification for the human aggression—to usher in the superior being—the *Uberman*, otherwise known as the *Superman*. He represented a master race, the most evolved form of human being, the most intelligent, most genetically superior, strongest being to ever exist. The Uberman was to walk this earth with a godlike quality, ruling all inferior beings and having the right and power to even determine who was to live and who was to die. These were the beliefs and teachings of a society which saw itself as divine.

One of these key tenets of the socialist mindset is to continually view and address issues through the dialectic perspective as presented and discussed in Observation No. 5: Socialists Lie. It was the single most driving force that propelled the nation into the seat as being the most evil and wicked empire of death. With Charles Darwin's book, *On the Origin of Species_by Means of Natural Selection, or the Preservation of Favored Races in the Struggle for Life*, there was a destiny for some form of evil in the world to eventually come and seek to fulfill what Darwin and others firmly believed in and advocated—the survival of the fittest humans. This hatred eventually manifested into the form of one single man of humble beginnings, about five feet nine inches tall but lived his latter days in godlike reverence—Adolf Hitler.

Still one of the most recognized faces of the modern world, Hitler was not a product of the German aristocracy nor had he been a person of renown within the hallowed halls of academia. The inspiration of evil was not a revered scientist nor did he impact the world of the fine arts or tantalize the world's stage with great wisdom. Determined to be an artist, Adolf Hitler was a very simple and basic man, in the beginning, but became a leader that people would be willing to die for. As a relatively quiet and insignificant fellow, he became a monster feared by kings and presidents. This man of relatively small stature eventually used his skills most destructively. He was able to convince the nation of German citizens as well as those of other nations and cultures that some groups of people were worth killing—it was for the betterment of humanity itself to exterminate the so-called *human vermin* to accelerate the continuing evolvement of those who deserved it. He became the god who established the morals for the Nazi war machine.

We know Hitler as having been the person who made the term *Nazi* a word to be feared throughout the world for generations. It is quickly associated with a type of person who brings death, especially those of different races. Today this term is often so easily thrown around by individuals without them having not even a clue of its meaning and purpose. The term stands for the National *Socialist* German Workers Party. Yes, socialism was the key driving force through which the German government managed the population. It was this system in which the bureaucrats and public officials were able to collect and gather the Jewish people and send them to concentration camps. In their quest to bring forth the Uberman, the Nazi government even launched a eugenics program that included removing from society their fellow German citizens, citing the idea that those who were considered to be *unfit* were institutionalized and forced to perform menial tasks if they were able so that they could at least earn their keep.

With the assistance of the American socialists, such as Margaret Sanger, the Nazis in Germany were well on the way toward purging itself of those that were considered to be "unfit." Sanitariums and institutions for the severely handicapped became avenues for eventual euthanasia. As Hitler and his followers encouraged German women to have more babies, non-desirables such as Jews, Slavs, and even German-born blacks and other inferior ethnicities were severely discouraged or worse. Although Hitler quickly turned against the socialist movement in Germany, they implemented some of the policies the socialists held as necessary, such as population control measures including birth control and sterilization, and when the system became stretched as far as they were willing to tolerate, they instituted a more stringent and deadly program aimed especially at the Jewish people, the Final Solution.

This program supported the intentional and purposeful act of committing genocide against any and all peoples that the Nazi regime considered subhuman. According to Darwin's Theory of Evolution, and Hitler's perspective, the white, blue-eyed, and blonde-haired Nordic person was the most evolved human, while the black and Jewish groups were the lowest forms of human beings.

"What then? If he be like to die, he had better do it and decrease the surplus population" is the heartless conclusion uttered about the possible plight of his underpaid worker Bob Cratchit's sickly son Tiny Tim by Ebenezer Scrooge in Charles Dickens's novella, *A Christmas Carol*. With this holiday season focused on fellowship, goodwill, and charity for the poor, Dickens's work was reflective of the British view of Christmas as it had basically become more of a drag on society instead of the time it was supposed to be. Perhaps the influence of the Enlightenment caused many to become callous and skeptical of this Christian tradition, but this and subsequent writings actually contributed to a revival of the Christmas holiday.

The character Ebenezer Scrooge's answer for Tiny Tim's sickness was for him to die and *decrease the surplus population*. This manner of thinking obviously came from the notion that there were too many people who were not contributing to the good of the population and production of goods but instead were more like parasites. Like Scrooge, socialism applauds the productive but despises the needy. In other words, it was better for society for those who were merely consumers of the general treasury to die—it would be less of a burden on the producers. Only those who contribute to the system should benefit from it. You must be compliant and submissive, but the ones who ask questions and insist that they have individual rights to refuse if necessary are dangerous and expendable.

If we were to consider the plight of many of the hundreds of thousands of individuals and families who are literally imprisoned in our inner cities, we see that incomparable death rates with very little compassion from those who benefit from them the most—the politicians. There are unbridled numbers of shootings and killings among our children and young adults, with hardly any signs of remorse or sympathy unless the shooting happens to have been committed by a white policeman. Then national attention comes with a vengeance! Then is the publicity and money that can be generated. All indications seem to declare an empathic "Yes!"

Take the city of Chicago, Illinois, for example. Every weekend and holiday may have some form of good and exciting news that highlights something that is newsworthy enough to elevate the spirits in celebration of the event. If the Bears were to win the Super Bowl, or the Cubs or White Sox, the World Series. Perhaps the Bulls happen to find their next Michael Jordan! There could be an event or an occurrence that causes an entire city to celebrate and unify like no other time in history.

However, if any of these wonderful events were to occur, the good news would most likely be overshadowed by the tragic news of an innocent child being mercilessly gunned down on a Chicago street! Too often, parents in Chicago, as well as many other cities, do all that they can to protect their young from flying bullets and the violent street culture in any way imaginable but still suffer the horrible tragedy of a child killed by a stray bullet. As communities scream in anguish, politicians make promises to make it better but quickly retreat back to the safety and quietness of the office and screen out the calls of those they had just promised. Perhaps they, like Ebenezer Scrooge, truly believe that decreasing the surplus population *does* make things better, but unbeknownst to the parents, the loss of a child meets their definition.

Chicago, Illinois, is one city where weekly, and sometimes daily, reports and statistical updates alert us to the truth that something is terribly wrong within many of our inner cities in particular—very wrong with the way many of us look at one another. Violent gunshot deaths of young people ranging from infants to young adults keep us on edge. Chicago's problem is not unique but is one of the leading cities in America. We suspect that sinister and wicked forces are in play here because the majority of us still do not accept the loss of precious lives without much effort to at least place a tourniquet on the flow of blood from our communities' arteries. However, as families wail in the agonizing pain of not just losing a child but doing so in such a brutally senseless way! Bullets coming through bedroom windows or even walls striking children as they slept peacefully in their beds. Little girls sitting on the front steps or porch of their home getting caught up in drive-by shootings. Young boys walking along a street or on a sidewalk killed simply because they were there.

Is there a legitimately common denominator? Sufficient evidence emphatically says, "Yes!" In a collective sense, each of these population centers of poverty and avoidable death is governed by liberal socialists, and they need victims just as much as the air they breathe! "We need the children to die as a sacrifice for the cause for greater gun control," their actions and attitude tells us. The violence within our cities must continue because keeping the inhabitants paralyzed in fear makes it easier to control them and dependent upon us. Fear and hatred are interchangeable. First, the people are taught to fear, which quickly converts to hatred for those they are convinced to be the cause.

In this case, gun control is the target. Removing firearms from private ownership is a key and necessary component of socialistic ideology in spite of what the Second Amendment guarantees. Therefore, there must be a class of victims—even babies and children—to be killed *not* by law-abiding gun owners, but by gang members and criminals who possess guns illegally. When people are no longer able to defend their lives, preserve their liberty, and protect their own property, the quality of life diminishes. Socialism's success ensures that the population becomes more dependent upon the governmental system, not only becomes the sole provider, but also the almighty protector. This is why children are dying, to saturate the public conscious to the point that there comes such an outcry to confiscate all firearms in spite of the US Constitution!

In the Marxist model, the value of human life is not based upon whether the individual has a God-given soul as well as a genuine, basic human right to life, liberty, and the pursuit of happiness, but is determined by one's ability to contribute or bring benefit to the system's order. The senseless slaughter of our children on the streets are of no value to the socialist model because their deaths cannot be used to further its cause for absolute government control, with the exception of gun control. People exist for the benefit of the state and are considered to be the property of the same, and because in the secular view, the morality of God is not valid because it is the morality of man which prevails.

The result of socialism's influence is therefore the eventual rendering of each human life as being less than or equal to any other living creature, and subject to eradication or extermination once that life loses its value to the system. From early youth, each person is taught to believe that his or her life's value is based upon the ability to contribute to the system, but when to individual becomes too old to contribute or physically impaired beyond the ability to function, the better solution would be to cease being a burden upon the state. The British babies Alfie Evans (May 9, 2016–April 28, 2018) and Charlie Gard (August 4, 2016–July 28, 2017) were born with serious genetic ailments where they were deprived of any and all lifesaving attempts but were allowed to die because the amounts of money budgeted for their treatments were exceeded. Even in spite of pleadings and offers from other countries and medical centers to continue treatments and offer rays of hope to prolong their lives and possibly find cures. The unfortunately final solution for both children was death.

However, the world was offering, if not a medical cure, moral and spiritual hope. In spite of the interest in treatment by American hospitals and Pope Francis's pleas for the hospital officials to release Charlie for treatment in Italy, the answer was a consistent no. Who rejects hope when it is offered in love and compassion? Apparently, those who seek to keep their system intact.

Besides, the wealthy have traveled from continent to continent seeking cures and treatments for whatever ails them. In many cases, they fly to places in the world that may offer something as insignificant as a tummy tuck, gastric bypass surgery, or buttock injections. When we view such items in comparison to what these two infants and untold numbers of others suffer from. Were the British officials afraid of possibly finding a cure or a type of technology or therapy that would have prolonged their lives in a sufficient degree of viability? Or is it through the socialistic perspective to simply *do the right thing* and die? Within the socialistic ideology, the apparent solution to the problem is to eliminate the person instead of finding the cure.

There is a form of *patriotism* that calls for the citizen to seek euthanasia when they are no longer a productive worker (taxpayer). One would wonder if the system were more content to simply continue to manage the lives of its citizenry from cradle to grave instead of researching for cures and health-related solutions that prolong them.

When the COVID-19 pandemic began to spread across the planet like wildfire, every nation sought to protect its citizenry from its dreaded effects. First of all, credible reports told the world that the Chinese government banned all *intracity* travel. This abruptly halted all travel from city-to-city whether automobile, bus, train, airline or anything else. On the other hand, the government allowed international travel. According to those who miraculously escaped from this prison nation, one of the ways the Chinese government handled individuals and families that contracted the virus was to force them into their apartments and welded their doors shut, sealing them to die slow and horrible deaths. This cruel and barbaric act resulted in mass starvation and certain death of untold numbers of perfectly innocent people—socialism's final solution.

Shanghai, a city of 25 million people, was quarantined to the point where residents were simply locked and sealed into their dwellings for weeks. The nights were filled with shrieks and screams by those residents, making the scene comparable to some sort of ghostly horror movie. They were managed and threatened by government health officials dressed in white hazmat suits and known as "Big Whites."

Now many questions follow the terrifying aftermath about the actual source and cause not just the spread of the virus, but its actual creation or evolution.

With the deaths of both Charlie Gard and Alfie Evans, the one thing that the people of Great Britain and the European Union itself should have realized is that there is a fence—a boundary that locks them in. Any population that lives as dependents under the *benevolence* of the socialist system have to someday come face to face with the truth that their freedom has seriously dire limitations, especially when the efforts to sustain the basic right to life extends beyond the prescribed barriers. The most common barrier is economic. The next one is when the medical knowledge of the culture cannot address the condition, followed closely by the limitation in medical technology. Is it the seriousness of the illness? Will it be old age (or young) that compels the authorities to say, "It's just time for you to die"?

The socialist system becomes overburdened by the very promises it is supposed to keep. The courtship assurances of health care, income, food, security as well as many and other various commitments.

During the eight years of former president Barak Obama's administration, there was one thing that also became known—Dr. Ezekiel's philosophy on who deserves health care. Dr. Ezekiel Emanuel, health adviser to President Barack Obama, is under scrutiny. As a bioethicist, he has written extensively about who should get medical care, who should decide, and whose life is worth saving. Dr. Emanuel is part of a school of thought that redefines a physician's duty, insisting that it includes working for the greater good of society instead of focusing only on a patient's needs. Many physicians find that view dangerous, and most Americans are likely to agree.[29] He is also one of the architects of America's Affordable Care Act.

According to this particular train of thought, an individual's value to the system (government) can determine his or her quality of life, including medical treatment, whenever applicable. With Ezekiel's rise to the limelight in the Obama administration, there also emerged the term "death panels" where it was believed that the life of a patient would ultimately be in the hands of a team of medical experts and professionals, with their decision becoming the final decision—somewhat like Evans and Gard.

Then Emanuel was quickly associated with what was known as the Healthcare Rationing Chart, which featured a graph with charted age as compared to productivity —especially in terms of paying income taxes. For example, it is obvious that infants do not and cannot work and are definite consumers of goods and services. Senior

---

[29] Betsy McCaughey, "Obama's Health Rationer-in-Chief White House Healthcare Adviser Ezekiel Emanuel Blames the Hippocratic Oath for the 'Overuse' of Medical Care," *Wall Street Journal*, Aug. 27, 2009.

citizens, who were most productive during their middle years, retire and cease productivity and become consumers of goods and services. Then the question is asked, "Who should receive the most of health care?" According to the principles of socialism, a person should have a finite time and financial allotment for health care from cradle to grave.

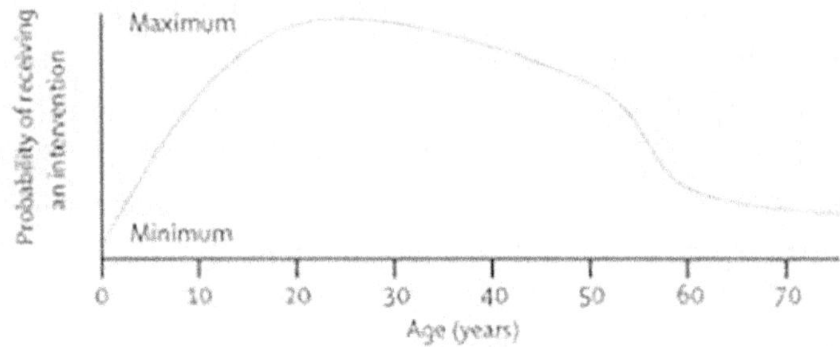

The Healthcare Rationing Chart provides a visible picture of how services are to be receiving services.

Why do the heathen rage, and the people imagine a vain thing? The kings of the earth set themselves, and the rulers take counsel together, against the Lord, and against his anointed, saying, "Let us break their bands asunder, and cast away their cords from us." (Psalm 2:1–3)

Final Conclusion

Socialism is incompatible with the American Dream which inspires the individual—whether native born or an immigrant setting feet on this soil for the very first time—to use those God-given gifts within them to be prosperous and successful in every way possible. Rejecting the principles that declare we are the property of the government and embracing that we were created by God with rights to life, liberty, and a pursuit of happiness, there can be no place nor system that proposes otherwise.

On the same hand, liberty and freedom actually require greater responsibility than that which socialism as well as communism mandates. Under our flag of liberty and freedom, we also have the responsibility to conduct ourselves in such a way that ensures a safe and stable system of government conducive to the well-being of all. Those codes for correct and proper behavior are found in the Holy Bible. If one refuses to believe in those teachings, may it be suggested to at least recognize, honor, and respect those principles as a continuing assurance for maintaining an orderly society. The quest to honor *nature and nature's God* does not have to be a religious commitment or endeavor for these principles are transcendent and universal to all people. Our problems began and yet continues as leaders felt that there was no longer the need to honor God nor his statutes.

Romans 13 of the Bible lays down the purpose and duty of government that has been "ordained of God." In other words, men did not create true and real government—God did. As he intended it to be, government's primary purposes were to protect the good and punish the bad—the lawful verses the unlawful. As the Founding Fathers described this duty "to secure these rights, Governments are instituted among Men, deriving their just powers from the consent of the governed." Socialism requires much more!

It can be compared to a river. It has natural boundaries as it courses its way through the terrain, twisting and turning, bobbing and weaving as it flows toward the sea. It makes these turns because it governed and guided by the river's boundaries. This is the way our US Constitution relates to our government. It provides the boundaries that govern and control its course of flow.

However, there are times when extremely heavy rains occur. Flood waters cause the river to rise up and out of its natural boundaries and wreak havoc upon the areas along its banks, causing damage and destruction. Similarly, when our government is allowed to rise up and above its Constitutional boundaries, much damage to those who live close it is done. This is us!

Socialism always proposes that government do increasingly more for the people than it should. Estranged from God, void of morals and pretending to be kind and benevolent, socialism's proponents use the resources of others to express *their* good—again, not of themselves but of others. Former British Prime Minister Margaret Thatcher is yet remembered for saying, "The problem with socialism is that you eventually run out of other people's money." Yes, socialists on the most part do not give nor contribute of themselves but will fight to the last person to get it from others to give to you. This is not what goodness is comprised of. Self-sacrifice does not require the sacrifice of others first!

Greatness and heroism are rooted in one's willingness to give themselves up for the sake of the greater good. Take for instance another example the Founding Fathers' unselfish act in signing the Declaration of Independence. Knowing that they were actually signing their own death warrants, they so courageously wrote in the closing statement, "And for the support of this Declaration, with a firm reliance on the protection of divine Providence, we mutually pledge to each other our Lives, our Fortunes and our sacred Honor." In other words, true heroes see the value in others being greater than even themselves, thus are willing to sacrifice for them. On the other hand, the socialists see themselves worthier to live than those they fight for but will sacrifice them for the cause. Socialists will always need victims to further their cause, and if they cannot identify any, they will create some!

The 118th Congress of the United States of America has a record low approval rating of an anemic 19 percent. This means that the American people have a very low opinion of them, their work, and their status as people who are expected to manage the nation's business. A key charge is that they are untrustworthy liars who do not want the American public to know the truth about their motives and their actions. If you have ever watched on TV a congressional hearing or investigation, you probably have witnessed the dialogues of some of the most elusive and deceptive conversations on earth. One single politician can spend hours shamelessly spinning half-truths and fables without any indication of regret or remorse. Socialists cannot tell the people they represent (with an exception for a few) that they actually are working to transform America into a place similar to Russia or China. For this reason, they have to lie and deceive. This makes lying a high-maintenance activity. Yes, lies are always high maintenance!

The most effective way to *fundamentally transform* this nation is to use various situations, conditions, and events to present them as being the reason and cause for *change*. Change to what? Socialism, of course! Use the situations to justify the need to cede power and authority to the government agencies in order to address and *solve* the problem. Climate change? Tell the people that the hurricanes and tornados are being made more powerful and intense because of climate change. Say that the droughts and the wildfires are the result of the same. The man who has been credited with developing a philosophy about successfully creating and telling lies in order to further an agenda was Nazi Germany's Joseph Goebbels. To manipulate and control the German people, he was known to have been the one who made propaganda an artform.

Though some credit Goebbels for the following statement, others doubt that he did. In either case, the Germans were successful in producing false information just the same. This is what Goebbels is credited with saying, "If you tell a lie big enough and keep repeating it, people will eventually come to believe it. The lie can be maintained only for such time as the State can shield the people from the political, economic and/or military consequences of the lie. It thus becomes vitally important for the State to use all of its powers to repress dissent, for the truth is the mortal enemy of the lie, and thus by extension, the truth is the greatest enemy of the State." Another possible quote attributed to Goebbels is shorter but still as descriptive, "Make the lie big, make it simple, keep saying it, and eventually, they will believe it."

Lies have always been high maintenance. They never can stand alone for any period of time because the truth will always chip away at its core until suspicion takes hold to prove its falsity. Thus, those who introduced it must always return and plaster it over with another lie, or at least a partial, to keep it standing. Then there eventually comes another and then another challenge, over and over. A lie cannot stand under the weight of its own facade and cover. Someone will always be there to inspect and then challenge its validity. This is why lies must always be worked on and maintained. The greater the lie, the greater the costs in terms of money, time, material, and manpower. Lies are expensive to maintain.